SPACE CLEARING

SPACE CLEARING

how to purify and create harmony in your home

Denise Linn

CB
CONTEMPORARY BOOKS

Photographers: Sandra Lane, Shona Wood
Styling: Ruth Prentice
Editor: Nicky Thompson
Designer: Ruth Prentice

This book was first published in Great Britain in 2000 by Ebury Press, Random
House, 20 Vauxhall Bridge Road, London SW1V 2SA.

This edition first published in the United States in 2000 by Contemporary Books
A division of NTC/Contemporary Publishing Group, Inc.
4255 West Touhy Avenue, Lincolnwood (Chicago), Illinois 60712-1975 U.S.A.
Printed and bound in Singapore by Tien Wah Press
International Standard Book Number: 0-8092-9739-6
00 01 02 03 04 05   19 18 17 16 15 14 13 12 11 10 9 8 7 6 5 4 3 2 1

Contents

Foreword

Every space has energy. Your home is not only a composite of materials assembled for shelter. Every cubic centimeter of it, whether solid or seemingly empty space, is composed of infinite energy. When you enter a space that makes you immediately feel light or uplifted, or walk into a room where the atmosphere leaves you feeling depleted and drained, you are responding to the energy of the environment. If you notice tension and heaviness in a room after an argument has taken place, you are experiencing a residual energy that can linger in a room long after the argument has ended.

Sometimes energy in a home or office can become stagnant and dull. When this is the case, you may feel tired and listless, or become agitated and angry. However, learning a few simple techniques to cleanse the energy of your home can produce a remarkable and positive influence on the way you feel, and on every aspect of your life.

For the last 30 years, I have practiced the art of cleansing and harmonizing home energy, a skill which I named "Space Clearing;" some people call it "home healing," "smudging" or "home harmonizing." No matter what name is used, present-day Space Clearing techniques have their source in ancient techniques practiced throughout human history. The methods and tools have varied from one culture to another, but the intent has been the same – to create greater harmony and balance.

Native Americans used drums, rattles and burning herbs in their rituals, while the Chinese used gongs, chanting, and incense. In medieval Europe, salt and prayers cleared energy, and in the Middle East smoldering resins such as frankincense and myrrh were used to invite blessings into a home.

These forgotten ceremonies that brought vitality to human structures generations ago are once again being used to instill peace and equilibrium in today's homes and businesses. Many people are finding that these ancient rituals can be adapted very successfully for modern day use, and most important, they are discovering that they work.

Traditional western businesses are hiring professional Space Clearers because they have found that doing so increases their sales and productivity. Some of the largest real estate firms are now using the services of Space Clearers in order to dramatically accelerate property sales. Land management corporations are employing Space Clearers to perform blessings on land before they build housing developments. People who had never heard of Space Clearing a year ago are now ringing bells, burning sage, and chanting mantras because they have found that their homes feel better as a result.

Space Clearing can have an enormous impact on every aspect of your life. When you call for blessings and assistance from the unseen realm of Spirit, untold magic and joy can fill your heart so that your house becomes a home for your soul.

OBJECTS GATHERED IN PREPARATION FOR A SPACE CLEARING: A RATTLE, TURKEY FEATHER, BUNDLED

SAGE AND LOOSE HERBS FOR BURNING; A MANDALA MADE OF OBSIDIAN AND ONYX FOR GROUNDING;

AND A DECORATED BAG FILLED WITH BUNDLES OF RESINS AND SALT FOR PURIFICATION.

CHAPTER ONE

Rebirth of an Ancient Tradition

The shaman slowly reaches forward to light the incense. As smoke fills the air, he begins a sonorous chant. The rising and falling of his voice seems to undulate throughout the room. Wave after wave of low humming tones flow from him, resonating into every niche and corner of the space. The soft beating of a drum accompanies his chant as he stands to face each of the four directions, asking for blessings for the home and all its occupants. In each direction he prays to the Creator for good health, prosperity, and love for all. The smoke settles. The drumming subsides. Everyone smiles. Good fortune will reign in this home.

For thousands of years, in ancient civilizations and native cultures throughout the world, sacred ceremonies have been performed to instill beneficial energy into living spaces. Although many of these traditions have withered in the climate of a technological world, arising from the deep wisdom of the earth comes the rebirth of Space Clearing. Forgotten ceremonies that once brought vitality to human structures generations ago are now being used to establish or bring peace and equilibrium in today's homes and businesses with remarkable results. Homes that felt sluggish or depressing become vibrant and uplifting after a Space Clearing. Stores and offices that have been cleared often report an increase in sales and morale. A room that is cleansed feels at once lighter and brighter – and even people not sensitive to energy remark how great they feel.

Space Clearing today can provide keys to inviting the natural world into our homes. It can reveal the spiritual possibilities lying dormant in our surroundings, dispel negative energy, and call Spirit and love into our homes and businesses. A home that has been purified not only feels better but sometimes, in seemly mystical ways, health improves, relationships deepen and prosperity expands. Ancient people understood the power of cleansing and blessing their homes and living structures, and this is why Space Clearing was such an important part of their everyday life.

The journey to understanding Space Clearing (and learning how it can make a difference in your home) lies in the realm of energy. Our homes are not just inanimate physical structures. They are receptacles for vibrating unseen energy fields which respond to human thought and intention. In this book I have sought to unravel some of the mysteries of energy and Space Clearing to show you how, when it has been cleared, the house becomes an environment of spiritual revival and inner poise.

When Space Clearing is needed

Space Clearing can be done at any time, yet there are particular moments when it is especially important to clear and bless your environment. The type of clearing that you do will depend on the history of the space and what has occurred there. For example, after a sickness or death of a loved one, the energy of a home often becomes sluggish and heavy, or *yin* in nature. To dispel the listless energy and restore balance in the area, clearing techniques that are vibrant and quick moving are required – these are *yang* in nature. Drums and gongs are excellent tools to use in such a case. On the other hand, if the energy of your space feels agitated, the use of *yin* techniques and tools, such as a softly chanted mantra or a crystal singing bowl, can smooth and soothe the energy to create tranquillity and calm.

Before construction of a new home

In ancient traditions, it was considered a sacrilege to begin the construction of a building before clearing and consecrating the land. Anecdotal evidence supports the validity of this belief, as homes built on battle sites or hallowed ground have often been plagued with continuous problems. Simply taking the time to connect and communicate with the earth, clearing the land of residual energy and offering blessings can make an enormous difference in the fortunes of all the occupants of a home. Blessings for the land forge a symbolic link between the house and the life-giving earth it rests upon. The occupants of the home will reap the benefits of living in this location.

Before moving into a home

In many cultures it was unthinkable to move into a home before it had been Space Cleared and blessed. Homes which have not been freed of energies sometimes continue to foster patterns of behavior related to the fortunes of the previous occupants.

For example, it is not uncommon for a business to go bankrupt in a building that has seen a previous bankruptcy. Although this may be attributed to a bad location, it is more likely that the negative energy generated by the previous misfortune creates a template for failure. Even if the previous homeowners were healthy, prosperous and happy, it is still wise to clear the space so you are free to create your own traditions and space in your new home or business. You will then be surrounded by your own energy rather than someone else's.

After misfortune

After illness, divorce, death or misfortune, it is absolutely essential that you Space Clear your home. Doing this facilitates a timely release of pain, suffering, sorrow, and discomfort, so that you can begin anew. It will literally help to "clear the air" of stagnant, unhealthy, negative, or unhappy energy. You should also Space Clear your home after arguments, home accidents or the departure of an unpleasant visitor.

Any time you need a lift

Space Clearing is also effective any time you need a lift in life. Have you been feeling sluggish or lack-luster? If so, this would be an excellent time to perform a Space Clearing ceremony. Although a complete clearing involves an entire home or office, even the simple act of lighting a candle, misting a room or ringing a bell will have a positive effect on how you feel, if it is done with the intent of transforming the energy in your environment. You may want to do a light Space Clearing every morning to start your day with crisp, clear energy. Simply walking around each major room in your home ringing a bell, lighting incense at an altar, or wafting the smoke of burning sage with a feather in the morning hours can set a template of clarity for the rest of the day.

Before a celebration or rite of passage

Space Clearing before bringing a new baby home, the arrival of an honored guest, or a rite of passage such as a marriage ceremony in the home, sets a template of clarity and light. It creates a perfect environment for generating fresh new beginnings.

The best times to Space Clear

Annual spring clearing

At least once a year, it is valuable to cleanse and purify the energy of your home. This will "set" the energy for the coming year. Ideally this complete clearing is done either at the winter solstice or in very early spring. Both times are auspicious for new beginnings. In the springtime, as new life abounds, clarify your goals and dreams for that coming year and then thoroughly purify your home and office top to bottom to create a powerful template for the coming year. Your Space Clearing ritual creates an energy that will continue to feed and nourish your home for the coming year.

The most auspicious time of day

Space Clearing can be done at any time of day or night; however, the early morning hours (especially after a waxing full moon the night before) offer the freshest and most potent energy. Opening windows and allowing morning sunshine to stream in during a clearing can invite beneficial vibrant energy into a dwelling. In Eastern European traditions, Space Clearings are often done at night during the dark of the moon. In these countries it is believed that disturbing or negative home energy is at an ebb at that time, so in theory it is easier to set a new energy in place.

CHAPTER TWO

Creating Sanctuary

When you cleanse and purify the energy in your home, it is transformed into a sanctuary – a retreat from the discord of the world, a place of refuge and protection. It becomes an anchoring point from which you venture out into the world and a welcoming abode for your return. A home that has been cleansed and blessed becomes somewhere you feel safe enough to be yourself, a place to embrace your joy and explore your pain. Space Clearing can turn every part of your home into a sanctuary of sacred space that nurtures the soul.

There are four steps in Space Clearing: Preparation, Purification, Invocation, and Preservation. Each step, taken with care and love, can contribute to bringing balance into your home and creating a powerful integration of your outer and inner life. The ceremonies and tools described later in this book can be adapted to these steps.

Step 1 Preparation

The success of any journey depends on the care and attention given to preparations made at its outset. There is immense power in beginnings for as the seed is nurtured, so grows the tree. Taking the time to prepare yourself, your tools and the space you are clearing will dictate how powerful the transformation will be.

PREPARING YOURSELF

The strength of your Space Clearing depends on your ability to intuitively sense energy, clarify your intention, and project your will into a space.

Developing your Space Clearing intuition

Your intuition is the key that will open the door into the revealing world of energy in your home or business. One way to develop your intuition is to spend time being absolutely still in nature. Only when you learn to silence your thoughts can your inner voices be heard, and this is easier in a natural environment. All Space Clearing has its roots in shamanism, and shamanism has its basis in a deep attunement to the natural cycles of nature. So to develop your intuition, spend time out of doors. Lie down on the earth. Feel her energy radiate through your body. Look up to the heavens. Watch the clouds as they form and make new shapes above you. Notice any signs or messages in what you see. Doing this exercise helps you to develop your intuition for perceiving the hidden messages you will find inside houses and offices.

Sensing energy

One of the skills necessary for Space Clearing is the ability to sense energy fields. When you have developed this awareness, you will be able to sense when energy is out of balance in a room and what changes must be made in order to restore harmony. To develop this skill, walk around the periphery of a space very slowly with one hand extended. Notice places where you feel a difference – your arm may feel heavy or light, warm or cold. There may be places that seem to feel sticky and others that feel smooth. This is not your imagination. You are sensing energy. The secret is to slow down, still your mind, and trust what you are perceiving.

Clarifying your intention

Where intention goes, energy flows. Before you begin any Space Clearing it is essential that you become very certain about what you hope to accomplish in a dwelling. The clarity and vigor of your intention will determine the direction and focus of the clearing. If your intention is to create a calming energy, this is what will occur. If you resolve that your Space Clearing will bring a dynamic vitality to a household that has been stagnant, then this will be the outcome.

Projecting your will

The more chi (inner energy) that you have, the more powerful your Space Clearing will be. When your chi is flowing, you can project your intention into a space magnificently and gracefully. To develop your chi you might consider practicing meditation or taking tai chi or yoga classes. An exercise to activate this unseen, yet very real, inner life force is to imagine that you have a ball of energy in your hands. Slowly move this energy ball around. After a while you should feel an increasing sensation in your palms. This is your chi increasing. Then, to

project your will into a space, imagine that your body is a sacred vessel and that vast loving energies of the universe are pouring through your hands into your home.

Protecting yourself

There is a mystical dimension within each of us wherein dwells the entire universe. It is a domain where you are not separate from the mountains, clouds or great seas. Ancient sages and visionaries have spoken of this dimension with awe and reverence. On a very deep level, there is nothing that is separate from you, so there is no need to protect yourself because everything is "you." It is not uncommon to enter this state when Space Clearing, in which case you do not need protection.

However, as it is not always possible to maintain this feeling of unity and oneness with the space around you, you may want to imagine yourself surrounded by a golden sphere of sacred space. This will provide you with a personal protective shield while you are working. You may also want to wear a religious or spiritual amulet while you work, or perhaps put a small amount of salt in your pockets – this is grounding and offers you protection while you work.

Cleansing yourself

Before you purify and bless a dwelling, it is essential that you cleanse yourself. If possible, bathe or shower, and wash your hair. If you can't wash your hair, then at least stroke water over the top of your head. Traditionally, cleansing of the top of the head allows for an unclouded connection between you

and Spirit. Your clothes should be clean, carefully chosen, and appropriate for the occasion (not casual, everyday clothes). For beginners, pastel clear shades or even white are often best because of the reflective nature of light colors.

Your state of mind

It is important when you do any Space Clearing that you feel mentally and emotionally balanced. If you feel any apprehension or fear about it, you should postpone your clearing until you feel confident and relaxed. If you are pregnant or menstruating, you need to tune in to yourself to see if your energy is right for a Space Clearing. A woman's moon time and pregnancy are times when her energy naturally turns inward. When doing Space Clearing you need to project energy outward. The Space Clearing techniques described in this book are completely safe for everyday use in your home. However, you should not attempt advanced techniques, such as the release of an earthbound spirit, without the assistance of a qualified professional.

PREPARING YOUR TOOLS

The tools that you use for Space Clearing are only a vehicle for your intention and prayers. By themselves, they cannot sanctify a home. Your bell, drum, or gong serves only as a focal point for you to direct energy into a space.

Choosing a Space Clearing tool

Choosing a tool for Space Clearing is very personal. One individual might fall in love with the frame drum and find that every time they hear its sound, they can sense energy more perceptively. Someone else might find that burning incense resins, such as frankincense and myrrh, creates a powerful shift of consciousness in a space. The best Space Clearing tool is the one to which you feel most attracted. How much you pay for it or where it came from does not matter as much as your love for it. A tool that is loved will be a powerful ally in your quest to bring harmony into living spaces.

Empowering your Space Clearing tools

To empower your Space Clearing tool, hold it close to your body and visualize it becoming an extension of your body and soul. When you and your Space Clearing instruments are thus attuned to each other, a special kind of alchemy is created which will strengthen every Space Clearing ceremony that you perform.

Giving your Space Clearing tool a name further facilitates its effectiveness. Naming is a powerful and magical act. In ancient cultures an instrument used for ceremonies was always revered and named. Words structure reality and whenever you name something you develop a much more intimate connection with it. Mentally addressing your Space Clearing tool by its name, before you use it, will automatically call forth stronger, more resonant energy.

Cleansing your Space Clearing tools

Before and after Space Clearing, cleanse all the objects that you use. For example, if you use quartz crystals, place them in the sun, or run clear cold

THE TIBETAN BELL AND ACCOMPANYING DORJE
ARE USED AS A PAIR FOR SPACE CLEARING.
TOGETHER THEY REPRESENT THE UNITY OF THE
YIN AND YANG FORCES OF THE UNIVERSE.

water over them so they are purified. A drum, bell or feather can be held in the smoke, over smoldering sage leaves or cedar needles, for cleansing. Shake out altar cloths and wash incense burners. Then place your Space Clearing things somewhere special where they will stay clean. This is important because it keeps a freshness and vitality around them.

PREPARING THE SPACE

The most powerful Space Clearing occurs in a place that has been physically cleaned and cleared of clutter. Clutter clearing is modern day alchemy. It is one of the fastest ways to transform your life and shift energy in a space. Clutter is any accumulation of things that impede the flow of energy in your home. Anything that you don't use or love can be considered clutter. As a suggestion, before any major Space Clearing of your home, go through each room removing as much clutter as possible. Get rid of piles of magazines you will never read. Transplant or throw away plants that are dying or dead. Repair or throw out anything that has been broken for a long time or has parts missing. In addition, do a thorough cleaning. Vacuum the rugs, mop the floors, wash the windows. Open the windows wide to allow sunshine and fresh air to fill your home. All this will contribute to making the Space Clearing more potent.

TO CLEANSE A FEATHER,
HOLD IT OVER SMOLDERING
SAGE LEAVES BURNING IN AN
ABALONE SHELL.

Preparation on the day

1 On the morning of your clearing, meditate for 12 minutes on the task before you. To do this, sit quietly, close your eyes and visualize your home space as being joyous, shimmering, and light.

2 Drink plenty of water, preferably spring water rather than from the tap. It is vital that you are properly hydrated before, during, and after the Space Clearing. The water will help transport energy through your body and will help release any unneeded energy that you may have taken on during the clearing.

3 Cleanse yourself. Pay particular attention to the top of your head.

4 Put food away in cupboards. It is best not to leave open containers of food out during the clearing as they may absorb some of the energy being cleared.

5 Tidy and clean the space thoroughly, if this has not already been done.

6 It is best to remove jewelry, particularly rings and bracelets. These can subtly impede your ability to sense energy.

7 Talk to other members of the household about their intention for themselves and the home that they hope to achieve through the Space Clearing.

8 Focus your intention on the results you desire for the home, the occupants and yourself.

9 Prepare flower offerings (see page 42). Flowers are often used in Space Clearing ceremonies because they bring a feeling of freshness and are thought to call forth blessings of the angels. Traditionally, flowers used for Space Clearing should be picked first thing in the morning as the sun is just rising. Each flower should be picked with care and thanks should be given to the plant for its gift.

In Hindu traditions the fragrance of the flowers used for blessing ceremonies should not be inhaled when they are picked. It is said that the first scent should be reserved for the Creator. If you are not so fortunate to have a garden, or it is winter time, then store-bought flowers are fine. Usually the best for flower offerings are carnations, calendulas, and marigolds because of their compact shape and durability.

10 Make sure animals are out of the space. The wagging tail of a friendly dog can send Space Clearing tools flying!

11 Set up your Blessing Altar (see page 36) with your Space Clearing tools and altar objects.

12 Offer prayers at the Blessing Altar for the success of your Space Clearing ceremony.

Step 2 Purification

The second step in Space Clearing is purification. It is during this stage that you release negativity and clear out old energy. Here is how you do this:

1 At the completion of your prayers, place any tools you will be using on a small tray (called a Blessing Tray) so you can take them safely with you from room to room. For example, if you plan to use a bell, a chime, a bowl of salt, and a small glass-enclosed votive candle for your Space Clearing ceremonies, place all these items on your tray. Any kind of tray is suitable so long as it provides a stable surface for your clearing items and is easy to carry.

2 Place the Blessing Tray in the area that you are going to clear. Then stand at the entrance of the room and take a few minutes to become attuned to the space. Radiate your intention into the room, and send prayers to the Creator for guidance and assistance.

3 Sensitize your hands. Breathe slowly and deeply. Sense the energy of the space. Circle the room with your hands extended, or use any of your senses to perceive the energy in the room.

4 Using the tool(s) that you have chosen, gradually break up the stagnant energy. As a general rule, circle the room clockwise in the northern hemisphere and counter-clockwise in the southern hemisphere, unless your intuition directs you otherwise. (In Mecca pilgrims go counter-clockwise around their sacred stone enshrined in the Kaaba. Buddhists walk clockwise around stupas.) Generally it is good to work your way from the bottom floors of a building to the top floors, as this directs the energy upwards.

5 After you have cleared each room, smooth the energy of the space. To do this, run your hand gently around the periphery of the room, just as though you were petting a cat, until you sense that it feels settled and smooth.

6 Remember to silence your mind, and go slowly with each step of the Space Clearing. This allows you to perceive subtle energy flows.

THIS BLESSING TRAY CONTAINS A NUMBER OF THE ITEMS FOR A SPACE CLEARING INCLUDING A CANDLE, A FLOWER OFFERING, INCENSE, SAGE, SALT, FRANKINCENSE, AN ANIMAL TOTEM, AND A FLOWER-TOPPED BELL FOR CLEANSING AND PURIFYING.

Step 3 Invocation

The invocation stage in a Space Clearing ceremony entails calling on a higher power for assistance, support, and inspiration for filling a living space with blessings. If you think of the purification stage of Space Clearing as being like washing a dirty vase, the invocation stage can be compared to placing beautiful fresh flowers in the vase. Here are the steps for this:

1 When you have finished clearing a room, imagine that it is filled with light and love while asking for support and guidance from the spiritual realms. You can pray silently or aloud to do this.

2 Stand in the door and make the sign of a figure eight (the sign of infinity) with your hand or your Space Clearing tool to seal the energy in the room and complete your clearing. The sign can be either horizontal or vertical.

3 When you have Space Cleared all the rooms, cleanse and bless each household member. This is essential because it aligns their energy with the newly cleansed energy of the home.

4 Return to the Blessing Altar. Offer thanks and ask for good fortune for the home and all its occupants and visitors. This is the most important aspect of the clearing and must be done with reverence, respect, and devotion. The length of time that this takes may vary. Usually the completion Blessing Ceremony lasts for about 10 minutes, but it may last longer depending on individual needs.

5 Wash your hands with cool water all the way to the elbows. Shake a few times before you dry your hands.

PLACING SPECIAL OBJECTS IN A ROOM, SUCH AS THIS LARGE BURMESE BUDDHA, CREATES A FEELING OF SACREDNESS WITHIN A HOME.

Step 4 Preservation

Once you have purified a space and then blessed it, it is valuable to preserve the wonderful energy that you have created. Here are a few methods:

1 You might want to "plant a prayer." To do this, write a prayer or blessing on a piece of paper during your completion at the Blessing Altar and bury it in a favorite plant. Every time the plant is watered, the prayer will be symbolically energized. You might also draw a symbol or write a special word on a stone either to place by the front door or by a plant. Placing a figurine of an angel, an object from the Blessing Altar or some other representation of the divine realms in a special place can also help to preserve the beautiful, cleared energy.

2 Everyone – you and all members of the household – should bathe within six hours after the Space Clearing. Doing this not only cleanses the body; it also symbolically refreshes the spirit and helps preserve the energy you have created. Bathing in salt water is especially beneficial. To create a salt bath, dissolve ½ lb (225g) of regular salt or Epsom salts to the bath water. If no bathtub is available, rub your body with salt before showering, ending with a cold rinse.

PLANTING A PRAYER: "PAX" (LATIN FOR PEACE) HAS BEEN WRITTEN ON A STONE AND PLACED IN A FLOWER POT.

CHAPTER THREE

Blessing Altar

The purpose of the Blessing Altar

Creating a Blessing Altar for your Space Clearing ritual provides a spiritual backdrop so that every action has meaning and power. The ceremonies performed within this sacred space deepen the overall effect of your Space Clearing. To create a Blessing Altar, arrange the objects that you will be use in your clearing rites on an altar cloth. This temporary altar serves as a beginning point and ending point for your ceremony. It has three purposes, and is perhaps the single most important aspect of Space Clearing. First, it initiates energy for the clearing. It is here that you call upon spiritual assistance and support. Secondly, it acts as a center point to radiate a protective, loving energy throughout the home during the entire Space Clearing. Finally, the Blessing Altar integrates the new energy that is generated by your clearing ceremony.

1 CALLING FOR SPIRITUAL ASSISTANCE

Beginnings are important, and the initiation of any Space Clearing is a sacred time. If you start clearing a house or office without first taking the proper steps, your ceremonies will not be as profound and powerful as they could have been. Your Blessing Altar is the place where you begin your ritual, open your heart, and call for spiritual guidance. Angels, spirit guides and guardians, ancestors, and totem allies respond and send beneficial healing energy when prayers are sent straight from the heart.

2 GENERATING AND ANCHORING ENERGY

The Blessing Altar creates a vortex of energy for the clearing. It becomes a sacred center from which you can draw energy as you work throughout the home. It also helps anchor and strengthen you.

Every object on the altar, as well as the placement of these objects, is meaningful. How you organize the altar creates a template for the rest of your ceremony and so the overall intention for your Space Clearing should be reflected in your Blessing Altar. For example, if your intention is to bring more love into a home, you may want to use a pink altar

A BLESSING ALTAR FOR LOVE
Each object here helps call loving energy into a home. The rose color of the altar cloth symbolizes warmth and affection. Spring flowers bring a feeling of freshness, vitality, and new hope for love. The shells in the mandala represent clarity of emotions. The sage and salt is for purification of any blockages to love and romance. The bell and white feathers are to invoke love and romance into the home. The two small bowls of salt and rice are for grounding and abundance.

cloth adorned with a mandala made of rose quartz pebbles. Fragrant rose petals sprinkled on the altar, pastel pink candles, an oil burner with ylang ylang, rose, or neroli essential oil would all help to generate the energy of your clearing, since all these objects are symbols of love.

3 GROUNDING AND INTEGRATING ENERGY

The completion ceremony performed at the Blessing Altar is as significant as the ceremony at the beginning, because it integrates the energy in the home. *If a Space Clearing is done without grounding and integration then disruption and turmoil can occur afterwards.*

Space Clearing without integration can be compared to the process of continually stirring up a stagnant pond: the water will appear disrupted and murky. Space Clearing can stir up old energy and it can make an environment feel disturbed and agitated afterwards. However, when energy is integrated at the conclusion of a Space Clearing, churned up energy in the home is smoothed into gentle flowing energy. It becomes like a stream of fresh water gently flowing into a stagnant pond, which eventually turns clear, without turmoil. Similarly, a grounded Space Clearing creates clarity and harmony throughout the home without undue disruption.

The completion ceremony at the Blessing Altar grounds the energy of the home and prevents a sense of upheaval afterwards. Without this integration, it is not uncommon for repressed energy to rise to the surface. For example, if a couple are harboring deep, festering anger and resentment, Space Clearing can result in turmoil and even loud arguments after the clearing unless there is a grounding. Space Clearing removes stagnant energy, which may be suppressing negative energy, so the process can be like lancing a boil. Old issues can rise to the surface after an ungrounded Space Clearing. However, when there is an integration ceremony at the Blessing Altar, a home will be filled with clearer, more balanced energy. This way hidden issues can rise to the surface in a safer and more harmonious manner, rather than through upheaval.

A Space Clearing without integration can sometimes also cause problems in the house itself, such as water pipes breaking or fuses blowing out. To avoid emotional or physical disruptions after a Space Clearing, please spend time at your Blessing Altar serenely sending forth prayers for the home and its occupants.

A BLESSING ALTAR FOR PEACE
The objects in this Blessing Altar are dedicated to instilling a peaceful energy into a home during a Space Clearing. The deep blue of the altar cloth represents peace and serenity. The quartz crystals on the right are for clarity and equanimity. The fluorite eggs on the left are for clearing and equanimity, the cornflowers symbolize calmness, and the Buddha is for inner peace. The chime and feather are for clearing and invoking a feeling of tranquillity, and the swirl of shells represents the great spiraling life-force energy of the Creator.

Creating your Blessing Altar

The care that goes into a Blessing Altar can positively impact an entire home. Carefully chosen objects placed on your altar in a deliberate and conscious way can create a mystic center of powerful energy that ripples in all directions. The first step is to become clear about your overall intention for the entire house. Decide what altar objects would best symbolize this. Your intuition will be your guide in your selection. Listed here and on the next few pages are some of the qualities commonly associated with various objects. These lists are a guide to get you started and are by no means complete. Symbols and their interpretations vary widely from culture to culture around the world. Use what works for you.

The color of your altar cloth and altar objects

Color impacts us physically, emotionally and spiritually, and your response to light is deeply ingrained in your nervous system. Because consciousness is so closely related to the spectrum of light, the color of your altar cloth will dramatically affect the energy of your Space Clearing. Here are some color associations to consider:

BLACK visionary, introspection, germinating, silence, and stillness   BLUE inner peace, inspiration, creativity, patience, spiritual understanding, faith, and devotion   GREEN balance, harmony, peace, hope, growth, and healing   ORANGE optimism, expansiveness, emotional balance, confidence, self-motivation, enthusiasm, and community   PINK love and softness   PURPLE spiritual perspective, intuition, calming, soothing, and comforting   RED strength, courage, steadfastness, health, vigor, passion, and sensuality. Revitalizing and stimulating, red can assist in overcoming inertia, depression, fear or melancholy.   YELLOW heightened expression, freedom, joy, clarity of thought, organization, attention to detail.   WHITE purity, clarity, and transformation

A BLESSING ALTAR DEDICATED TO SPIRITUAL RENEWAL
The purple altar cloth and amethyst crystal wands symbolize spirituality, the turquoise for opening the heart and crown chakras, the sea salt and incense resins provide spiritual cleansing, the rice is for spiritual abundance, the white shells and flower represent spiritual purity, and the candle is for inner light.

Flower offerings

Flower offerings are a simple, elegant expression of love, beauty, and Spirit – and a perfect way to seal the energy of each room. Once you have cleared a room, leave a flower offering in a place where it will not be disturbed by people or animals.

To make a flower offering, place a small votive candle (that come in metal containers) in the center of a heat-resistant plate, saucer, or dish. (Take care never to light a candle so near to flammable materials that they might catch fire.) Arrange the flowers around the candle. Use colors and flowers that are appropriate to your overall intention. To energize your arrangement, take the head of one flower and use it to sprinkle holy water (see Chapter Six) gently over the other flowers in the offering. You can also place a stick of incense in the candle wax, or in an incense holder, next to the offering. Ideally, these offerings should be left in all the major rooms of the home after a Space Clearing for at least 24 hours.

These offerings are also a way of giving thanks to the Creator and the spirit guardians for their love and assistance, and they honor the four sacred elements. Incense honors the Spirit of the Air, flowers acknowledge the Spirit of the Earth, the candle represents the Spirit of Fire, and the holy water venerates the Spirit of Water. When your offerings have served their purpose, return them to nature with a prayer of thanks.

SPRING FLOWERS IN A FLOWER
OFFERING SYMBOLIZE NEW BEGINNINGS.

Stones and gemstones on your Blessing Altar

Polished stones and gemstones have been used on altars since the earliest times. It was felt that each type of stone or gem could elicit a particular and unique kind of energy. Some activated healing, others were used for soothing and relaxing, while others were used to evoke vitality. Using specially chosen stones or metals on your Blessing Altar can quicken the specific kind of energy associated with them. Here are some qualities generally associated with common gems and stones:

ADVENTURINE healing   AGATE success, happiness   AMBER protection, healing   AMETHYST compassion, clairvoyance   AQUAMARINE harmony   BLOODSTONE healing, physical strengthening   CARNELIAN physical grounding   CITRINE mental clarity   EMERALD spiritual healing   FLUORITE mental attunement, calming GARNET physical strength, assertiveness   JADE healing, wisdom   LAPIS spirituality, intuition, royalty MALACHITE psychic power, healing, cleansing   MOONSTONE emotional balancing, lunar qualities OBSIDIAN grounding   OPAL emotional clarity   PERIDOT mental and physical healing, rejuvenation QUARTZ CRYSTAL spiritual attunement   RUBY strength, health, and spiritual passion   SAPPHIRE devotion, spirituality   SELENITE dreaming skills, intuition, meditation   TOPAZ expansion, knowledge TOURMALINE purification, healing   TURQUOISE healing, balancing

NATURAL STONES that you gather from special locations can be sources of healing energy for Space Clearing. Similarly, a stone given to you by someone special to you will contain the energy of that connection. Placing these stones on your Blessing Altar is one way of implanting their energy into the space.

Plant and flower offerings

On altars throughout the world, you will find offerings of fruit, flowers, and grains. These are traditionally used because they represent the bounty brought forth from Mother Earth. A glowing orange, a small bowl of rice, a beautiful arrangement of bright flowers – all of these things add richness, beauty, and a feeling of abundance to the Blessing Altar, as well as anywhere else they are placed in the home. They call in these qualities for your clearing, and can secure them into the energy of the home once your ceremony is complete. Flowers and plants are a wonderful way of generating energy for your Space Clearing. Here are a few varieties you can use and their associated qualities:

Flowers

CHRYSANTHEMUM introspection, meditation, longevity   DAFFODIL childlike joy, laughter
DAISY innocence, happiness   IRIS delicate sensuality   LILY purity, perfection
LILY OF THE VALLEY springtime, new life   MARIGOLD joy, longevity   ROSE love
SUNFLOWER optimism, joy   TULIP vitality, sensual love   VIOLET tenderness, trust

Fruits and grains

APPLE health, vitality   CORN harvest, abundance, fertility, blessing
GRAINS prosperity, renewal   MUSTARD SEED faith
PEACH immortality, marriage, tenderness
POMEGRANATE fertility, unity of diversity   RICE good fortune
WHEAT abundance, harvest intuition

Other offerings

When you are choosing items for your Blessing Altar it is
valuable to keep in mind the meaning that each item can
bring to the overall energy of the home. Here are just a
few of some commonly used offerings and their
meanings:

ASHES purification, regeneration
FIGURINES OF ANGELS, HOLY DEITIES OR ANIMAL
TOTEMS call forth spiritual assistance
REPRESENTATIONS OF THE FOUR SACRED ELEMENTS:
AIR (FEATHERS OR INCENSE) uplifting
WATER (HOLY WATER) cleansing and purifying
FIRE (CANDLES) transforming
EARTH (SAND, STONES OR SALT) grounding
SHELLS feminine energy, power of the sea and the moon
WINE blood of life, eternal life
WREATHS cycle of life

Essential oils and incense

An essential oil burner or a burning stick of incense can deepen the energy on a Blessing Altar.
Here is a list of a few natural essential oils and the energy they can contribute to your Space Clearing:

BERGAMOT uplifting, yet calming   CEDAR WOOD relaxing   CHAMOMILE soothing, calming
EUCALYPTUS invigorating, cleansing, tonifying   FENNEL relaxing, warming, calming   FIR NEEDLE refreshing,
cleansing   FRANKINCENSE calming, helps release fear, spiritual clarity   GERANIUM balancing mood swings,
harmonizing   JUNIPER purifying, stimulating   LAVENDER calming, soothing, relaxing   LEMON uplifting, refreshing,
mental alertness   LEMON GRASS stimulating, cleansing, tonifying   LIME invigorating, refreshing
MYRRH strengthening, inspiring   NEROLI stress reducing, calming   ORANGE uplifting, refreshing
PATCHOULI inspiring, sensuous   PINE refreshing, cleansing, stimulating   PEPPERMINT stimulating, cleansing,
refreshing, invigorating   ROSE emotionally soothing, loving   ROSEMARY stimulating, cleansing, invigorating
SAGE cleansing, purifying   SANDALWOOD spiritual attunement, helps release fear   THYME stimulating,
strengthening, activating   YLANG YLANG soothing, sensuous

Prayers at the Blessing Altar

BEFORE SPACE CLEARING

The best blessings come from your heart. When you call upon assistance from the divine realms, it will come. A simple prayer, straight from the heart, can prompt a wonderful sacred energy to fill you and the space that you are clearing. The words you use are less important than your intent. At the beginning of your Space Clearing you can either arrange your Space Clearing tools and altar objects in silence, or you can say a blessing for each item on your Blessing Altar. For example, as you place an offering bowl filled with rice on your altar cloth, you might say, *"I dedicate this offering of rice to abundance and prosperity for this home."*

After you have arranged the Blessing Altar, take a moment to center your thoughts. Then, either in silence or aloud, state your intention and ask for blessings for the home. An example of a prayer might be:

I dedicate this Space Clearing to love, joy, and good health. May harmony and peace embrace all the members of this family and may all who enter this place find comfort here. I humbly ask for spiritual guidance during this Space Clearing.

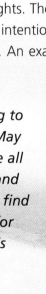

AFTER SPACE CLEARING

This is an example of a prayer you might use at the conclusion of your Space Clearing:

Creator, spiritual guardians and angels, thank you for the loving assistance that was given to us during this Space Clearing. Thank you for the peace and joy that is now flowing into this home. May the effects of this clearing and blessing continue for the months ahead, and may the wonderful, positive energy that has been instilled in this home bring comfort and rejuvenation to all.

CHAPTER FOUR

Sacred Sound

Sound has the mystical ability to restore harmony in objects, people, and environments. The results obtained are real and lasting. For this reason, sound has been highly valued for Space Clearing for thousands of years. In ancient cultures, sound was traditionally used to shift energy and to allow access to altered states of consciousness. In monasteries and temples throughout history, sacred sound has been used to create hallowed ground. Healers, shamans, priestesses and priests have also employed sound for healing, purification, and blessing rituals. You can use these same techniques to harmonize your home; however, you will find it valuable if you first understand the spiritual nature of sound.

An early creation myth of our planet states that all life began with primordial sound. As the sound spiraled round and round, it combined with matter to create the varying forms of animate and inanimate life on earth, and each form was imbued with its own sound. These ancient beliefs are consistent with the principles of modern physics which state that all atoms and molecules are in a constant state of movement, thus creating a resonance which can be described as a kind of sound vibration. It's as if each atom is singing its own unique song, which combines with the sounds of other atoms to create a collective harmonic.

When shamans speak of the "song of the grasses," they are referring to the fact that they can actually perceive all the silent – but very real – harmonic vibrations created in nature. They understand that there are two aspects of sound: audible sound and silent sound. Audible sound can touch our emotions and even create a physical vibration that can shatter glass. However, the most powerful sounds are those that are unheard. These can also be some of the most beautiful. Both audible and silent sounds are used in Space Clearing.

The energy of both of these kinds of sound surrounds you continuously. Each flower, stone, river – in fact, every single thing around us – has its own vibration. Even man-made objects have their own sound. The oak dresser, the antique rug, and the glass vase all have their unique sound vibrations. And when the vibration of a person, place, or thing is out of synchronization with its own innate rhythm, the result is discord. When sound is used as a Space Clearing tool, it can bring everything in a room back into harmony.

If you ring a bell or clap in a room that is out of balance, the sound will seem dull and muffled. After the negative energy of the room has been cleared, you can hear the difference: sounds will be crisper, sharper, and much clearer. When you use a musical instrument to cleanse the energy of an environment, the sounds created actually "tune" every board, brick, wall, and object within that environment.

Sound creates geometric forms. Photographs taken of fine powder placed on a membrane, while varying sounds are played, show the powder arranging itself into beautiful mandala-like formations and symbols. Changes in pitch and tone even cause some patterns to spiral in geometric configurations resembling kaleidoscopic images. The sounds created in Space Clearing utilize the energy imprints of these shapes, orchestrating a kind of synchronization and resonance that attunes the entire area.

Clearing a room using sound

Any musical instrument can be effective in Space Clearing. Your own voice, the clapping of your hands, a simple reed flute, or an instrument you have made yourself can all be used. The single most important consideration is the personal connection you feel to the instrument you have chosen. A tool that is loved will emanate a strong and vibrant energy. A tool that means nothing to you, or one that is treated carelessly will not be as effective, no matter how much it cost or where it came from.

Sound alone cannot harmonize the energy in a room. It is the magical combination of sound, empowered by your intention, that creates a miraculous shift of energy. Effective Space Clearing happens when your heart is open and your intention is clear – only then can you project your energy through your tool.

Before your clearing, hold your instrument close to you and imagine your energy merging with its spirit. Enter into the realm where it becomes a part of you. As you create a sound, shift your consciousness so you can feel it resonate inside you. Imagine sound radiating out from you to fill the room, tuning each corner and object. You are the conductor and every object in the room is being harmonized under your direction.

When using sound, it can be helpful to employ a range of sizes of the same instrument. For example, if you are using bells, you can begin with a large bell to break up the heavy, stagnant energy, and then move to a small bell to refine and distil fresh new energy. You might circle the room once with the larger bell and then again with the smaller, higher-pitched bell.

THE HIGH-PITCHED TONE OF A CHIME IS AN EXCELLENT WAY TO REFINE ENERGY IN A ROOM.

Clearing individuals using sound

Shamans have used sound for balancing and healing people's energy fields since prehistoric times. After you have cleared the energy of a home or office using sound, it is also valuable to attune the energy of the people who will be using the newly cleared space, so that their energy is aligned with it. This can be done with the individual in a sitting, standing, or supine position, depending on the personal preferences and comfort concerns of the person being cleared.

To clear a person's energy using sound, take your bell, singing bowl, gong, drum, tuning fork, or other sound instrument and create sounds as you move the instrument up and down the body. Make sure no loud sounds are made next to the ears as this can be uncomfortable. As you work, listen carefully to the sounds you are making. If you find any place where the sound seems more muffled or where you sense that energy is stuck, continue to concentrate sound in that area of the body until you feel the energy shift. If the person is lying down, you can magnify the energy of the sound by positioning stones or gems on the body in relation to the seven chakras.

You can also place stones, shells, or flowers in a ring around the person to create a circle of protective and healing energy. This will enhance the energy created by the sound work you are doing.

THE SEVEN CHAKRAS

1 On the floor above the head.

2 On the center of the forehead.

3 On the throat.

4 On the center of the chest.

5 On the diaphragm.

6 On the center of the abdomen.

7 On the floor at the base of the spine, or on the pubic bone.

PLACING STONES OR GEMS ON THE CHAKRAS, WHILE SPACE CLEARING AN INDIVIDUAL, WILL DEEPEN THE EFFECT OF THE CLEANSING.

Space Clearing instruments

BELLS

Bells have the ability to shatter accumulated stagnant energy by producing a sound that permeates the molecules of a space. The tone increases the flow of energy and restores vibrational balance. Concentric circles of sound continue to tone a room long after the sound has faded into silence.

Historically, bells have often been associated with mysticism. Ancient metalworkers believed that a kind of alchemy could be achieved during the bell-making process. In some cultures, bells were traditionally made of seven metals, each of which was thought to carry the energy of a different planet, an idea originally postulated by Aristotle. When such a bell was rung, it was believed that it generated universal forces capable of aligning the cosmos. Iron was associated with Mars because of its rusty red color and importance in ancient warfare. Lead, heavy and sluggish, was linked to Saturn. The metal mercury was associated with the planet Mercury because of its quick movements. Silver represented the moon, while the sun was linked to gold. Emperors like Holy Roman Emperor Rudolf II commissioned bells made of the seven hermetic metals, believing they would inspire tremendous energy.

TIBETAN BELLS AND DORJES IN VARYING SIZES.
THE LARGER BELLS BREAK UP STAGNANT ENERGY.
THE SMALLER BELL REFINES THE ENERGY.

Decorating your bell with flowers

In many traditions, the bell is honored by adorning it with flowers. Tibetan and Balinese bells have openings at the top through which you can intertwine flowers. Decorating your bell with flowers also adds the delicate energy of the flowers to your Space Clearing. On your Blessing Altar you may want to have a stand for your bell and this can be decorated with flowers as well.

In other traditions, the ringing of metal was thought to drive away harmful spirits and negative energy. Hebrew rabbis rang bells before entering the most sacred areas of a temple to keep negativity at bay. In Medieval Europe, church bells were rung not only to call people to worship but to dispel dark forces. At the same time that sacred bells were crafted and used in Europe, they were also being rung in the temples, monasteries, and ceremonies of Japan, China, Tibet, Indonesia, India, and Africa. In Buddhist cultures, the sound of the bell was an offering to Buddha, while Egyptian drawings on tomb walls also show priests ringing bells to bestow blessings.

Balinese bells

There are many different types of bells. Balinese bells are often used for Space Clearing because of their superior tone. Perhaps part of the power of these remarkable bells comes from the fact that their creation is synchronized with the phases of the moon; prayers and blessings to the gods are offered at each step of the process. Making a bell can take two months or longer, and on the auspicious day when it is finally completed a beautiful consecration ceremony calls life into the newborn bell.

Tibetan bells

Tibetan bells (ghanta) are excellent tools for Space Clearing. Although originally made in Tibet, since the Chinese took control of the region in the 18th century these highly symbolic bells have been made in India and Nepal by Tibetan refugees. Every part of a Tibetan bell is richly laden with meaning.

The bell always comes with a small metal object called a dorje which represents the male principle, power and salvation. The bell itself represents the feminine principle, wisdom and the great void. Using the ghanta and the dorje together is thought to restore balance in a room because they represent *yin* and *yang*, the two opposing, yet harmonious, forces in the universe. Their combination creates an inner mystical unity, a balance of the two primordial creative forces of life.

Sometimes, frightening faces are imprinted on the surface of Tibetan bells. These images of gods and goddesses are intended to dispel forces of evil and darkness. On the top of the bell is a mandala of eight lotus leaves symbolizing the voices of the gods. Along the bottom edge of the bell are images of 51 dorjes, representing 51 challenges that can be resolved by the ringing of the bell. Traditionally a lama would ring the bell while doing mudras (ritualistic gestures) with the dorje, which represented the dance of the gods. A Tibetan bell can also be played in the same manner as a singing bowl by circling a wooden mallet around its circumference (see page 59).

Other bells

The history and folklore surrounding bells could fill an entire book, and beautiful bells are made all around the world. Their sounds and the metals from which they are fashioned vary according to the traditions of their origin. Any bell can be used for Space Clearing if you feel a sense of connection with it and love its sound. Use your intuition to find the bell that is right for you.

TINGSHAWS

Tingshaws, or prayer chimes, are two small cymbals attached by a leather thong. Tibetan in origin, they have been used by Buddhist monks as well as in shamanistic traditions. Like Tibetan bells they are often decorated with symbolic patterns that affect the energy of the sound. Tingshaws are excellent for breaking up stagnant energy because they create a sharp piercing sound when struck at right angles to each other. They can also be used for smoothing the energy afterwards – dangle them by their cord and gently tap them together to produce a sound.

HARMONY BALLS

Harmony balls, sometimes called Druid balls or Mayan balls, are small metal balls filled with tiny metal beads that roll around inside to create a magical chiming sound. These are excellent for smoothing the energy of a space after Space Clearing. Cup the harmony balls in your hands and imagine they are filled with blessings for the entire household. Then take one in each hand and imagine that you are sprinkling stardust and light into the space as you shake them throughout the room. Magic!

CHIMES

Many manufacturers of wind chimes also make hand-held chimes for meditation or Space Clearing use (see page 56). Because of the focused precision of their sound, these are excellent to use in a bedroom, especially after an illness or if a couple hasn't been getting along. They are also great to use if you have been feeling unfocused and muddled in life, because they bring an energy of pure clarity and direct focus. When you use these chimes, you can sweep the walls (and the bed) in long, flowing movements. Long sweeping movements with chimes are also effective for clearing yourself or another person after Space Clearing.

TUNING FORKS

Whenever you use tuning forks you are producing pure musical resonance based on mathematical proportions known as Pythagorean tunings. These tones reflect the sonic ratios inherent in nature. The sound from tuning forks creates an archetypal resonance that results in a re-patterning of form and spirit. Tuning forks are remarkable for clearing wooden antiques or solid objects. Antiques often hold residual energy which may be negative in nature, so it is very important to clear them. Strike the tuning fork on your hand and then take the end of the fork and place it on the antique. You will hear the sound as it vibrates and travels along the grain of the wood. Continue to place the tuning fork on various places on the antique until you sense that the sound is clear. When choosing a tuning fork, listen to each one first to decide which one you are the most attuned to – this will be the best note for you to use for Space Clearing.

GONGS AND SINGING BOWLS

The use of singing bowls and gongs in Asia dates back to more than 3,000 years ago. Over time it was discovered that different metals created different energies in the sounds. The mixture of seven

specific metals – gold, silver, nickel, copper, iron, zinc, and antimony – was believed to create a unique and powerful energy. Many bells, gongs and singing bowls, especially in Tibet, were therefore created out of this combination of metals.

Some of the older gongs and singing bowls (those made before the Chinese takeover of Tibet) are said to contain iron ore extracted from meteorites.

Gongs come in the form of hanging gongs or bowl-shaped gongs, and are known for the sounds that seem to linger in the air long after they are struck. They are very powerful tools for creating sacred space.

Bowl gongs

As their name suggests, these gongs are shaped like a bowl. They range in size from 2–36 inches (10–90 cm) across. The resounding intensity that can be created when the wooden mallet strikes the rim is remarkable. It can feel as if it is vibrating deep into your core. Bowl gongs have a penetrating sound that lingers in the air long after they are struck. Tibetan bowl gongs contain the seven metals mentioned above and can be used as singing bowls as well as gongs. Chinese bowl gongs do not function as singing bowls, but they are the most durable of all the gongs and can usually retain their tone even after being dropped. Bowl gongs from Japan tend to be smaller than the Tibetan or Chinese gongs and therefore are excellent for travel. They create a very pure, clear tone.

Hanging gongs

Hanging gongs are used in temples throughout Asia as a call to worship. It is believed that if your spirit can truly follow the sound of the gong, you will reach God. Shaped like a large platter, hanging gongs usually range from 12–24 inches (30–60 cm) in diameter. The vigor and expanse of the sounds they create can clear a room instantly. Their ability to immediately break up and clear large amounts of negative energy make them perfect for using in very large spaces, such as an office complex or a warehouse.

Because many of these types of gongs are large, heavy, and difficult to move about, they do not adapt easily to the clearing of smaller rooms, although you can hang a large gong from a stand and place it at the Blessing Altar. You can use a small hanging gong in the center of the rooms you clear by holding it by its cord, striking it and then swinging it back and forth to send the sound in all directions through the room. In a very large open space, you can even swing the gong in circles over your head.

Clearing a room with a bowl gong

Place the bowl in your palm (if it is a small gong, place its small cushion in your palm with the gong resting on top of it). Whenever you enter a new room, strike the gong three times with your mallet to declare your intention. Walk around the periphery of the room striking once wherever you feel it is needed or whenever the sound fades. Continue to move the sound throughout the space until it feels clear.

SINGING BOWLS

Picture the following to help appreciate the effectiveness of a singing bowl. The monk cradles the large metal bowl in his hand. His fingers rest gently on the cold, smooth surface as the weight of the bowl lies heavy on his palm. Focused and deliberate, he strikes the rim with a wooden beater and slowly begins to circle its edge. A deep reverberating hum begins to build, powerfully and majestically. His eyes close. His breathing becomes slow and deep. Sound fills him until he experiences disappearing into the sound. Ripples of sound undulate through him and fill the room. Softly laying down the mallet, he sits quietly until the sound becomes a whisper…then stillness. Slowly opening his eyes, he looks at the space around him. The entire room seems to glisten with energy and light.

Tibetan singing bowls, sometimes called Himalayan bowls, come from Tibet, Nepal or northern India and have an outstanding ability to purify the energy in a home. These remarkable objects can create a sound vibration so powerful it can feel as if

the walls are coming down. The vibration of the sound seems to reach deep inside your soul. Some western doctors now use singing bowls with cancer patients because they have found the sounds produced can have an impact on diseased cells. When used for spiritual purposes, the sound of the singing bowl can also project powerful energy forms.

Alexandra David-Nèel, an intrepid French adventurer who spent 14 years exploring Tibet in the early 1900s, described an event in a remote lamasery when she saw flashes of light coming out of a singing bowl played by a lama. The holy man said the sound from the singing bowl could create shapes and even spiritual beings. He declared that one's thoughts and intention could travel on the sound of the singing bowl to create manifestations of energy.

How to make your bowl sing

Hold your gong close to your heart. Imagine filling it with love and heart energy until you feel as though you are merging with its spirit. When you are ready to play, hold the bowl in one hand. Keep your fingers free from the sides of the gong, or they will interfere with its sound. Gently tap the edge of the rim with the beater (this is said to "wake up" the bowl), and then slowly begin to circle the gong in an easy manner. Going quickly does not produce a better sound. Press firmly and evenly against the rim. If you press too lightly the stick will vibrate against the rim and cause a rattling sound. Allow the tone to increase in intensity. If there is an unpleasant sound of wood on metal, you can cover the part of your mallet that touches the metal with a strong smooth tape. With large singing bowls, sometimes rubbing the stick back and forth on a small section of the rim creates a more pleasing sound than circling the entire rim.

Clearing a room with a singing bowl

Slowly and carefully circle the room, holding the bowl in one hand while you are "singing" it with the other hand. Allow your entire body to be involved so that it becomes an extension of the singing bowl. Let your awareness travel on the sound to every part of the room. Visualize filling the space with vitality, light, and heartfelt energy. If there is a place where the sound seems dull or where the energy seems stagnant, continue singing the bowl in that area until the sound is clear and bright.

Choosing a gong or singing bowl

Don't be concerned about the beauty or symmetry of a gong or bowl when you first look at it. Regardless of its outward appearance, the gong that is meant to be yours will seem to emanate a unique inner beauty. Take the gong and hold it close to your heart chakra and gently strike it. If it is truly yours it will seem to resonate through your entire body.

When choosing a metal gong, some people prefer a hand-hammered one to a machine-made, symmetrical one. Although hand-hammered gongs are usually older, the sound and spirit of a new gong can equal an old one's. It is a matter of personal preference. Most metal gongs are sold by weight, so heavier ones will be more costly.

When you buy a singing bowl, it will usually come with a beater. This wooden mallet should be heavy and smooth, as the denser the wood and the smoother the surface, the better the tone produced in the bowl. You may also want to buy an additional beater covered with felt or leather so you can strike your gong rather than circling it. Different mallets will bring out different sounds from your gong or singing bowl, so you may find it useful to have a selection.

CRYSTAL SINGING BOWLS

Crystals have been used for spiritual practices for thousands of years, and have the ability to transmit information and energy (one reason why they are used in quartz radios). Quartz crystal singing bowls have a special ability to harmonize the subtle energy of light in a room. The energy they produce is almost alchemical in nature and can dramatically raise the consciousness of a space. Crystal bowls are best used where the energy of a space is already pristine and refined, such as in a meditation room or healing center. They are less effective for clearing very dense, heavy energy.

Crystal singing bowls range in size from 6–20 inches (15–50 cm) in diameter, and different sizes produce different tones. When selecting a bowl, let your intuition guide you to one that is best for you.

These ethereal-looking singing bowls can be played by gently tapping them with a padded wooden mallet to create a pure bell-like sound. You can also circle the circumference of the bowl with a rubber-coated mallet until it begins to sing. Be care-

ful not to allow the vibration to become too intense for too long, as this can crack the crystal. The spiraling movement of the sound creates mystic spirals in the energy of the room. Because of their delicate nature, crystal singing bowls are usually played at a Blessing Altar rather than carried around the room. Alternatively, you can place the bowl carefully in the center of each room and play it there.

To feel the mystic power of a crystal singing bowl, cradle it in your hand with the weight of the bowl on your extended palm. Focused and deliberate, strike the rim with a wooden beater and slowly begin to circle its edge. A deep reverberating hum will begin to build. Close your eyes and allow your breathing to become slow and deep. Feel the sound fill you. Imagine that you are disappearing into it. Sense ripples of sound undulating through you and filling the room. Softly put down the mallet and sit quietly until the sound becomes a whisper – then stillness. Open your eyes, and look at the space around you. The entire room should seem to glisten with energy and light.

Singing bowls and water

One remarkable way to use a singing bowl (metal or crystal) is to fill it part way with water. Ideally use holy water (see Chapter Six). This combines the energy and power of sound with the purifying quality of the Spirit of Water. When you circle the bowl with your mallet, the water will vibrate in small concentric patterns. Eventually small waves

A CRYSTAL SINGING BOWL CAN GENERATE A REMARKABLE SOUND THAT WILL PENETRATE EVERY PART OF A ROOM.

meet each other and tiny sparkling droplets jump up off the surface of the water making tiny fountains. You can keep adding water until you reach a pitch that feels right. This is a wonderful cleansing way to harmonize the energy in a room, and if you save the water from the bowl, you can use it later in a water cleansing ceremony. If the bowl is metal dry it thoroughly or it will have water stains.

OTHER MUSICAL INSTRUMENTS

Any instrument can be used for Space Clearing. A piano or harp played with a focused intention to clear a space can do a magnificent job, but an obvious limitation of large instruments is that you cannot carry them from room to room. However, with a strong intention a piano can clear an entire small wooden house as the sound penetrates through the wood. A flute, whether made of silver, wood or reed, is very well suited for Space Clearing. As with any tool, the most important elements are your focused attention and the attunement of your body to the spirit of the tool.

Anything that makes a pleasant, soothing, or even amusing sound can be effectively used in Space Clearing. Little "squeakies," the kind of toys made for babies or animals, although not technically musical instruments are nonetheless excellent for dispelling heavy or overly serious energy. They bring a spirit of laughter to a space and are very good for children's rooms or anywhere that you want to instill an atmosphere of fun and lighthearted joy. Laughter can also be an extraordinarily effective Space Clearing tool.

CLAPPING

You have no Space Clearing tools with you, and you need a quick fix right now? No problem. Use your hands! Walk around the circumference of the room with one hand extended to sense the energy. Any place where the energy feels stuck, give three swift claps. Sense the energy and then clap again to see if the energy has changed. The sound should be crisper and brighter the second time. Once the area is clear, take your hand and smooth the energy, and then continue round the room.

CHANTING

One of the most sacred uses of the human voice is for clearing and blessing a space. Since ancient times, when sages and mystics understood the great power of words, chants have been created to combine the powerful meaning of a word with a particular vibration of a sound. Indeed, chanting is such a powerful tool simply because it combines sound vibration with sacred words. You can follow this tradition by repetitively chanting words that have a special meaning for you. For example, you could chant the word "home" over and over again in your Space Clearing with the intention that each of the occupants of your household will feel at home with themselves wherever they are.

Om

One of the best-known examples of chanting is the use of the mantra, "Om." This powerful Sanskrit word signifies the sound of the Divine and the

THE SYMBOL "OM" REPRESENTS THE SACRED SOUND OF LIFE.

totality of all life. It is believed that this sound has the ability to release suffering and create profound transformation. To make this sound, simply relax, breathe, and gently exhale the sound "Ah-Ohhhh-Mmmm." Let yourself merge with the sound until you sense that you are filling the space around you. Go slowly. Allow the sound to find its own octave and rhythm.

Om mani padme hum

Pronounced "Ah-Ohhh-Mmm Mah-Nee Pad-May Hum," this Sanskrit mantra is translated as "the jewel in the lotus." It is believed that this combination of sound links you directly to the Creator, empowers anything that you do, and can activate compassion and love both within and around you.

OM The totality of all of life.
MANI The jewel symbolizing that which is of most precious value.
PADME The lotus rising out of darkness into the light as it moves up through the muddy pond. A symbol of awakening wisdom.
HUM This word awakens consciousness.

Because this mantra has the power to awaken spiritual forces within any space, it is an excellent way to end and begin any Space Clearing.

Hey-ya

Although there are over 400 Native American tribes in the United States, each with their own traditions and language, there is a mantra-like chant that is used in all tribes. This word, "hey-ya," calls Spirit, and is similar in sound and meaning to words used in other earth-based cultures around the world. A repetitive chant of "hey-ya" before, during, and after your Space Clearing can dispel stuck energy and call the natural forces of the earth into balance in a dwelling. The emphasis is on the "hey" with a forcible amount of air being projected as you say it.

TONING

Toning is the creation of tones or vowel-like sounds without the structure of a chant. It is a primal sound resonating through your entire body, and can be extraordinarily powerful. To tone, reach deep inside yourself to find your primal sound. It is that most essential sound within you, the quintessential expression of who you are.

One way to find your sound is to go up and down the musical scale, humming until you find a note that seems to resonate through your entire body. Once you have found this, stand in the middle of the room, open your mouth, and allow this single note to flow out from your body to fill the entire space. As you tone, you may find that the pitch of your sound spontaneously changes. Sometimes a room will respond to a lower note first, and then later you may find yourself using higher notes as the vibratory energy of the room rises. You will know when the space has been toned because it will feel balanced and calm. You can also tone an individual object in a room. Do this by bringing your mouth close to the item, and cup your hands by your mouth to direct the sound.

Tibetan prayer wheel

Mystical swirling Tibetan prayer wheels send out prayers of peace to the four corners of the universe. These wonderful tools, which were once only used in Tibetan monasteries as a way to send blessings to the world, are now being used by Space Clearers. At the top of an ornately decorated wooden handle rests a metal cylinder which contains thousands of hand-printed prayers. Every swirl of the wheel sends these prayers into the home. Spinning the prayer wheel as you chant is a very effective way of deepening the power of the chant. These are also excellent to use when blessing the land around a home.

RECORDED MUSIC

Sometimes music can be a helpful adjunct to Space Clearing. A very soothing melody, ambient music, or a sacred chanting CD or tape can form a powerful backdrop to the clearing that you are doing. It can help you remain focused while you work, and can even help balance the energy in an unoccupied room. However, there are times when music can distract your ability to sense energy fields, so it is important to be aware of whether the music is enhancing or detracting from your Space Clearing. You should be guided by your intuition to decide what is best.

DRUMS AND RATTLES FOR SPACE CLEARING

Drumming speaks to us directly of the basic rhythm of life. It re-creates that primordial pulse of life first known in the womb. In ancient times, drumming was used to sanctify and cleanse homes before moving in, and after sickness or death. Tibetan, Japanese, African, Chinese, Indonesian, Middle Eastern, Innuit, Saami, and Native American

cultures all have used the drum to bring harmony. The beating of a drum can align a living space to the universal tempo within all things.

Types of drum

The most common type of drum for Space Clearing is the frame drum, which is a hand-held drum about 12–15 inches (30–38 cm) in diameter. However, other kinds of drum, such as the African drum carried by a strap over the shoulders, can also be used.

Click sticks

In Australian aborigine tradition, click sticks are substituted for the drum. The rhythmic sound of click sticks produces the same shifts of energy as the sound of a drum. It is easy to make your own click sticks (also sometimes called clap sticks) from wooden dowels or any two sticks you find in nature. You can use them plain or you can sand them until they are smooth and then decorate them. They can be painted or carved with symbols that are sacred to you. The most important thing is the sound, which should be sharp and crisp.

How to use drums for Space Clearing

Different rhythms will produce different effects on you and the space you are clearing. Instead of deciding what tempo you want to use, let your drum tell you what to do! It will dictate the cadence, strength of beat and even which part of the drum surface to strike as you allow its energy to flow through you.

To begin, hold your drum close to your heart and imagine that you are breathing life into it. Hold an intention of your desire for your clearing. Then rub your hand around the surface of the drum to warm and greet it. If no rhythm emerges immediately, begin with a two-beat. This is the same rhythm as a heartbeat and will allow you to enter into a deeper state of consciousness where you can sense subtle energy.

As you start to walk around the perimeter of the room, notice any differences in the sound of the drum. If there are places where the sound is dull, pay attention to those areas, and keep drumming until the sound is clearer. Often, varied rhythms will spontaneously occur as you enter different areas of a room. You will intuitively find the exact rhythms that are needed for each part of the room.

Irish drums (bodhràns) can be used both for toning as well as rhythmic cadence. They have a magnificent ability to amplify the sound of your toning or chanting into a space. To use the bodhràn in this way, hold it close to your mouth without actually touching it. Cup your hand against your mouth directing the sound to the drum skin and begin to tone. The skin of the drum will vibrate with your sound, radiating the sound into the room.

Care of your drum

Drums should be stored in a dry area out of direct sunlight. The tension of the head of the drum will fluctuate in response to weather conditions: the humidity and heat in the air. If you live in a damp climate and your drum sounds a bit flat, this is natural. You may need to warm it gently in front of a fire or over a lamp, taking care not to burn the skin. If your drum sounds like a tin can, it may be too dry. In this case you can lightly mist it with water until the tone you desire is obtained. A drum should be kept in a place of honor, either hung securely on a wall, stored in a beautiful bag or case, or placed with its face up.

Rattles

Rattles are an excellent complement to the use of a drum in your Space Clearing ceremonies. While a drum is perfect for breaking up accumulated energy, the rattle is good for smoothing energy afterwards. It operates on the same principles as the drum but is more smoothing in nature. You can make your own rattles from plastic eggs which are usually sold around Easter. Fill them with seed beads (tiny decorative beads used in craft work). Close the eggs securely, and then decorate or paint them with patterns and colors that feel right to you. With these simple tools you can smooth the creases out of any space.

A SEED POD RATTLE, AN EAST INDIAN METAL RATTLE, AND A BEADED NATIVE AMERICAN RATTLE.

CHAPTER FIVE

Alchemy of Air and Fire

Fire and smoke have been used in religious rites since the dawn of time, and today they link our lives to those of our ancient ancestors. A candle's flame and the gentle plume of smoke rising from a stick of incense into the air are universal symbols of our connection to Spirit, archetypes recognized by people around the world.

Although different tribes and cultures may disagree about which herbs and rituals are best, nevertheless there is an abundance of similarities between the surface which transcend any differences. Fire burns away impurities, both physical and spiritual, while the trail of incense smoke carries prayers and supplications to the heavens. This duo has been used for thousands of years to purify and transform energy, to help people to enter an altered state of consciousness, and for the healing of bodies and minds. When you use the tools of fire and smoke in your Space Clearing work, you are embarking on an ancient tradition that can create a haven of balance, harmony, and healing.

THE TRANSFORMATIVE MAGIC OF FIRE

Since earliest times, man has been fascinated by fire. An essential ally in the struggle for survival, fire has sustained us, body and soul, from the beginning. Small wonder then that art, religion, dance, myth, and poetry have celebrated the amazing phenomenon of fire throughout the ages. Ceremonies using fire are some of the most powerful for instantly clearing the energy of an environment. Fire consumes, transforms, and destroys, even as it clears the way for the new. It is primal; pure energy, passion, transcendence, and inspiration.

When you begin your Space Clearing, place a candle on the Blessing Altar and keep it burning throughout your ceremony. The light and energy from this candle will be at the heart of all you do and will help you to manifest your intention. Before you start, take a moment to let your hands absorb the warmth of the candle's halo. Cup your fingers around the light and draw its spirit to your body. Focus on your intention for the clearing. Brush the fire energy over your head and body with light, quick movements to cleanse your aura.

You can purify the energy of your tools by holding them above the candle's flame (be sure not to hold them so close that they catch fire or become overheated). As you pass each tool through the purifying energy of the fire's warmth, let your intention center on your purpose for the clearing and the part that the tool will play in it.

You can also light a small votive candle in each room you clear. Allowing it to burn to extinction will deepen and set the energy that you have created there. An alternative option is to place a small votive in the center of a flower offering in each room (see page 42). Doing this combines the power of the fire's purifying energy with the gentle and beautiful energy of the flowers.

To turn an ordinary votive candle into an aromatherapy candle, light it and wait until the wax has become partially liquefied. Then blow it out and add a few drops of an essential oil to the liquid wax. Allow it to cool before putting it away to use at your clearing. This is an inexpensive alternative to more costly aromatherapy products.

I like to use beeswax candles whenever possible instead of petroleum-based paraffin candles. Although they are more expensive and can sometimes be difficult to obtain, they have a remarkably pure energy and high-frequency vibration. The delicate aroma they emit when they burn brings to a room all the golden clarity of amber honey, and the fresh energy generated by open fields full of herbs and flowers.

SPIRIT SMOKE

A delicate plume of smoke curling upwards through still air evokes immediate and powerful associations with ritual, purification, and spiritual connection. For thousands of years humans everywhere have burned herbs, scented wood, resins, and other aromatic substances as a way to channel their hopes, prayers, and dreams to the realm of Spirit.

Smoke purifies and transports. It transforms the ordinary into the sacred. It speaks directly to one of our most powerful and primordial senses, the sense of smell, a sense integrally connected to buried memories, emotions, and perception. Because of this connection, the use of smoke can powerfully and instantly change the energy in a room.

SMUDGING

In smudging, the smoke produced by burning herbs is used to purify and transform the energy of a space, to alter consciousness, or to clear the personal energy of yourself or another. Although the practice of smudging is pan-global, in the western world two of the most common herbs used for this purpose are sage and cedar, both of which are very potent purifiers. Sage is regularly used throughout the world as a powerful antidote to the energy residues left by illness.

Smudge bundles

Herbal sprigs bunched together and wrapped tightly with string are one of the easiest and most common ways to use herbs for smudging. The dried smudge bundle is first lit and then extinguished, leaving the still-smoldering herbs to give off their pungent smoke. (Please note cautions below concerning the use of burning herbs.)

Bundles of sage for smudging are easy to obtain through many mail-order businesses (see page 126), but the most powerful herbs to use are those that you have grown, gathered, and bundled yourself. Doing this provides a more intimate connection with the plant than is possible in any other way. Prayers are given at each stage of the process for the health of the plant and to thank it for its giveaway.

The best time to gather your own herbs for smudging is at dawn, when the sun is just peeking over the horizon. In that moment, slowly and deliberately walk toward the plant you have chosen. Kneel and give thanks for its gift to you. Then gently place your hands on the branch you have chosen to use for your ceremony. Ask permission from the plant to use a part of it, and then wait in silence until you sense that this permission is given. If you do not sense this, then move on to another plant and ask again. Never take more than a small

portion of a plant. It is essential to leave most of the plant so it continues to stay healthy. Also, offer a gift in return for what you are taking. In some traditions, a bit of hair or some cornmeal is offered to the plant and the soil while a prayer of thanksgiving is said. Herbs gathered in this way have a remarkable and unique power.

Loose herbs and pieces of resin

Sage and cedar in leaf form, frankincense, myrrh, and other resinous materials can also be used for smudging. To do this they must be burned in a fireproof bowl which is large enough to contain at least several inches of soil, sand or salt. The fireproof bowl must also be placed on some fireproof surface in the unlikely event that the heat causes it to crack.

First, light a small charcoal tablet or briquette with a candle or lighter and place it in the bowl. It is essential to use metal tongs when lighting the charcoal because it will become extremely hot very quickly. In addition, the part of the tongs in contact with your hands must be insulated with fabric or leather, because they too will become hot from the charcoal. The charcoal sometimes emits large sparks when you are lighting it, so be sure you light it in a safe place away from anything that could catch fire from a stray spark.

Once the charcoal tablet is burning in the fireproof bowl, you can place herbs or resinous incense on it with the tongs. Usually this creates a volume of smoke. Carefully carry the bowl into each room so that the smoke fills every corner of the home. Hold the thought that the smoke puri-

fies and blesses everything that it touches. It's important to be aware of smoke detectors, so switch these off or avoid moving under them while you are going from room to room.

Once you are complete with your ceremony, lift the charcoal briquette out of the bowl with your metal tongs and extinguish it in a container of water. A charcoal briquette and smoldering herbs can both appear to be out, but have been known to spontaneously re-ignite hours later, so caution about this is essential.

When you are burning loose herbs, it is best to let them burn simply by fanning them with a feather or fan. Do this carefully as movement can cause the smoldering leaves to fly out of the bowl, trailing embers into the room and thus creating a potential fire hazard.

A BURNING CHARCOAL TABLET, SMOLDERING IN AN ABALONE SHELL AND INSULATED IN SAND, NEEDS TO BE COVERED WITH HERBS OR RESINOUS INCENSE TO CREATE SMOKE FOR CLEARING.

INCENSE

Incense is a powerful ancient tool for Space Clearing. It has been universally used for large and small rituals, from the high mass of the Catholic church to the private use of incense on a personal altar. The smell of incense in a room can transform its mood and atmosphere, creating a sense of magic, and a connection to inner wisdom. In past times it was used before moving into a new home, and to disinfect a room after sickness or a death. Priests and priestesses burned incense before sacred ceremonies as a way to clear the space and invoke the gods.

The energy of incense varies with the place of its origin, the manner in which it is made, and its ingredients. It is important to use the purest quality incense you can obtain and afford, and to use incense that is made from natural rather than synthetic materials.

Incense is commonly made from various parts of plants, woods, tree resins, seeds, leaves, and evergreen needles. Each culture has its own special varieties – frankincense, myrrh, sandalwood, patchouli, cinnamon, cedar, and sage are some of the best known. Sticks, cones, leaves, resins, needles, pellets, and tablets – the forms which incense comes in are multitudinous. It can be fun to experiment with different kinds to see which you prefer and which ones work the best for the clearing work that you do. Here then is a brief glimpse into the dazzling, diverse world of incense. The ones listed below are only a tiny fraction of the varieties available from many cultures.

Indian incense

India is known as the Mother of Fragrances, so-called because of the incredible wealth of scents that are such a vital part of its culture. Probably the single most important incense out of all these myriad fragrances is sandalwood. Considered vital for the optimal passage of a soul from one life to the next, Ayurvedic medicine lists it as a remedy for many ailments. Sandalwood is excellent for bringing relaxation and peace into a home. Other Indian scents include elemi, common myrrh, benzoin, patchouli, and dammar.

Japanese incense

The Japanese have developed their practice of "listening to incense" over thousands of years. Elevated to the status of a great art form, an elaborate ceremony for savoring the pleasures of scent is called Koh-do, which translates as "the journey of the fragrance."

Although most of the ingredients of Japanese incense are not native to the country and are imported, the subtle blends and meticulous attention paid to the manufacture have made Japanese incense among the finest in the world. The most important source of scents in Koh culture is aloes wood, sometimes referred to as agar wood. Ancient records describe a piece of aloes wood washing up on the shore of Awaji island in the 6th century. The villagers did not recognize it as anything special and burned it along with other driftwood. But its fragrance was so startlingly lovely that it was taken and presented as a gift to the Empress. Since that time, aloes wood has been considered highly valuable for its enchanting aroma. Other common ingredients of Japanese incense include cinnamon, sandalwood, cloves, Japanese anise, and camphor.

Native American incense

Underlying the Native American use of plants for incense is the belief in the living spirit within all things. As the incense is burned, it is believed that the inherent wisdom within the plant is imparted to the person burning it. If the individual doing the Space Clearing has an open heart, secrets will be shared about what is good for her people, and what is needed for healing the dwelling. Thanks should be humbly offered to the spirit of the sage or cedar for gifts received. This is the Native American way of respect and harmony.

The smoke of the incense is also thought to carry prayers to Great Spirit, and is a channel for blessings to flow back to the earth. Thus the circle is completed. In a traditional Native American Space Clearing ceremony, sacred herbs are burned in a shell or piece of earthenware which is first offered to the sacred Four Directions: East, South, West, and North, before being used in the ritual. In this way the connection between people, the earth, and the spirits is honored. Tobacco, sage, sweet grass, cedar, and juniper are some of the herbs most commonly used for Native American incense ceremonies.

Middle Eastern incense resins

Steeped in mystery and historical significance, one of the most powerful cleansing resins is frankin-

cense. The tree it comes from grows in rocky desert (in a narrow strip of land only 9 miles long) that contains the exact minerals that give frankincense its delicate fragrance. This remarkable resin has unprecedented healing properties. It acts as a disinfectant that has been shown to kill bacteria and heal wounds. It is believed to have been used in temples, churches, and mosques because it reduced the risk of infection and disease when many people gathered together for services.

Some people develop an aversion to frankincense because it reminds them of church. This is

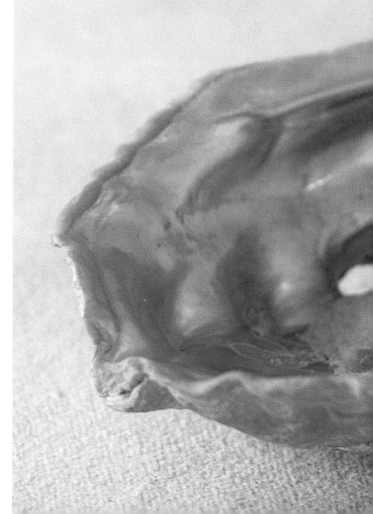

unfortunate because it is one of the strongest substances on our planet for cleansing a space. In addition, it can open subtle energy channels for spiritual and even cosmic energy to pour into an environment. Used in combination with myrrh (which was considered to have "feminine" energy while frankincense was considered "masculine") you have a most powerful combination to clear and bless a dwelling.

Before doing a Space Clearing it is valuable to cleanse yourself with smoke. To do this, light the herbs, smudge bundle, or resins and then cup your hands into the smoke and "wash" the smoke over your ears saying to yourself, "So that I may hear the truth." Over your closed eyes, "So that I may see the truth." Over your throat, "So that I may speak the truth" and over your chest, "So that my heart is opened during this Space Clearing."

FEATHERS

Beautiful companion of fire and smoke, the amazing feather – a symbol of power, grace, and freedom – has been a favorite tool of shamans since the beginning of human history. Because the quill of the feather is an open tube, many cultures have believed that it serves as a channel for energy and prayers. Energy moves through the body of a person, through the quill and is ultimately channeled directly to the Creator. A multitude of blessings flows in return from this ultimate source back down through the center of the feather and into the heart of the one holding it.

Because of its delicate attunement to the finer aspects of energy, feathers are useful for all phases of Space Clearing, from the initial assessment to the clearing and balancing of energy. Many people

Every feather has its own unique energy, and knowing the qualities of each bird that it comes from will let you use them to best advantage in your clearing. Please note that governments often have very specific legal restrictions regulating the possession of bird feathers. These laws are intended to protect species which might otherwise become extinct. Out of respect for these creatures and our environment, it is essential that you first check what regulations relate to possession and use of feathers in your area. The following is a list of just a few feathers and their attributes. When you are trying to decide if a particular feather is right for you, tune into its energy.
Let your intuition tell you what is best.

EAGLE AND HAWK Soaring and powerful, these invoke the energy of the sun.
GOOSE Geese mate for life, and live in highly socialized flocks, so their feathers are linked to loyalty and family ties.
OWL An owl feather invokes the energy of the moon and is associated with wisdom and ancient mysteries.
RAVEN Linked to the inner life and secret realms, this has a powerful and ancient energy.
TURKEY An excellent feather for Space Clearing. In native tradition, it is considered to be the "giveaway bird," because it gives its life for the benefit of others. This energy will greatly enhance your work as you provide the service of Space Clearing for the benefit of those around you.

have found that it is easier to assess the energy of a room, object, or person using a feather than with their hands alone. This is because the subtle nature of the feather's own energy makes it able to tune into the finest shifts of energy in the environment. The feather allows you to tune into levels of aware-ness which may have previously been inaccessible to you. If your intention is clearly focused, with a single feather you can clear an entire home.

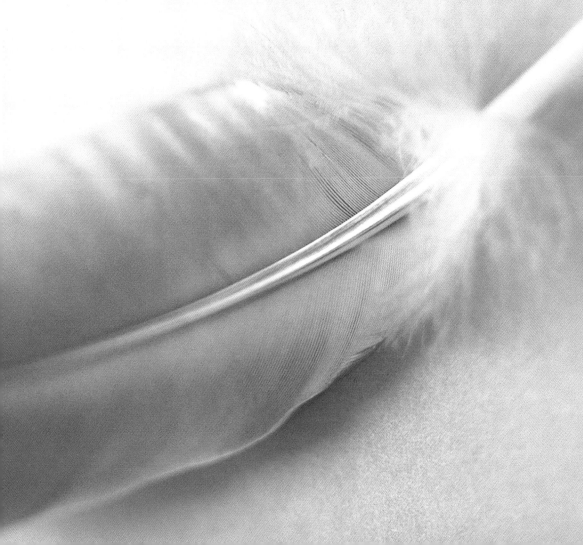

Caring for feathers

Keep the feathers you use for Space Clearing in a cherished place. Treating your feathers with the respect they deserve enhances their effectiveness. You will want to "feed" your feathers by occasionally dusting them with a bit of cornmeal and then flicking it off. Doing this symbolically feeds the spirit of the bird from which the feather came, and replenishes the feather's energy.

Many birds have insect parasites which may be present in feathers. If left untreated, these mites will eventually eat your feathers away and destroy their beauty and usefulness. Storing your feathers in an airtight box in the freezer will prevent this, as will storing them in cedar, sage, borax, or tobacco.

Types of feathers for Space Clearing

There are three traditional forms of feathers for Space Clearing: single feathers, feather fans, and wings. A single unadorned feather is an excellent tool for Space Clearing. You can also decorate a feather by wrapping the exposed end of the quill with leather or cloth. This in turn can be decorated with beads and strips of leather.

A feather fan is usually made from several feathers gathered together and secured with a piece of leather or a wooden base. The feather fan has a wider surface for moving energy throughout a room. Like single feathers, fans can also be made very beautiful with a variety of decorative methods, from painting and beading to exquisite embroidery and leather work.

When you are using an entire wing from a bird, it will usually be from a goose or turkey, as these are more easily obtained. Occasionally you may come across a raven or owl wing, although of course whenever you are working with wings from wild birds, the above noted restrictions must be respected. It is also very important to make sure that the wing has been properly cured and treated for insect infestation before use. Wings move air and energy in a very powerful way, as well as being beautiful. They call to mind angelic energy, and are associated with angels.

Using feathers with smoke

A traditional and highly effective way to clear a room is to combine the movements of the feather with the use of smoke. This is one of the most powerful ways to balance the energy of any room. The natural channeling powers of the feather, combined with the healing spiritual properties of the burning incense or herbs, can create a sense of sacred space in a very deep and immediate way.

To clear a room or a person with a feather and smoke, hold a bowl containing sand and the smoking herbs/incense in your non-dominant hand. Make sure that the bowl is deep enough to prevent any sparks flying out of it into the room. You must also make sure that the bowl contains enough sand so that it does not become so hot that it burns your hand. Use the feather in your dominant hand to move the smoke over the body of a person or throughout a room. Use the same movements as described above – small, flicking motions followed by long sweeping ones. The beauty of the plumes of smoke being moved about in this way can be very healing.

Cleansing your aura with smoke

Place a bowl of smoking herbs or incense on a table, and then draw the smoke to your body with a feather or your cupped hands to cleanse and purify your aura before beginning your clearing. Clear your mind and focus clearly on your intention as you draw the smoke down the body.

Clearing a person's aura with a feather

When using a feather to clear your own energy or that of someone else, you will want to begin by holding the feather next to your heart, and imagine yourself merging with the spirit of the bird from which it came. As you become one, together you will work to achieve the magic of the clearing.

Start by using short flicking movements, going from head to toe over the entire body of the individual. Whenever you sense that there is stagnant energy in a place (this will feel "sticky" or somehow just "wrong" as you move the feather along), then concentrate your efforts there with short quick movements to break up the stagnant energy. Once you feel the energy beginning to move, switch to long strokes of the feather to smooth out the energy and increase its balanced flow.

Clearing a room with feathers

The same principles apply to clearing a room with a feather as to a person. Begin with short, flicking movements as you circle the room in a clockwise direction (in the northern hemisphere – go counterclockwise in the southern). Wherever you sense a pooling of stagnant energy, chop into it with the feather to break it up. Then make your motions with the feather longer, slower, and more fluid to encourage the influx of a healthy flow of balanced, calm energy into the room.

"BREATH OF GOD"

One powerful Space Clearing ceremony that utilizes the alchemy of air is the shamanistic technique of "breathing a room," which is sometimes called the "Breath of God." To use this potent technique, imagine that you are breathing in life force energy with every breath. Then, as you slowly move about a room, if you find an area which seems murky or full of stagnant energy, you can use a series of short, quick breaths blown out through your mouth directly at the area that feels stuck. Once you have broken up the stagnant energy in this way, you can use long, out-flowing breaths to smooth and refine the energy. Your hands follow the movement of air created by your breathing to enhance the effectiveness of this Space Clearing technique.

FANS

In some cultures, fans made of bamboo, wood, paper or woven grasses were used for Space Clearing. If you are unable to obtain feathers or choose not to use them, fans can be employed in the same manner. In ancient China, women used fans to avert negative energies, and with a subtle twist of the wrist flicked away negative energy. To use this type of fan for Space Clearing, use swift concise movements.

CHAPTER SIX

Holy Water

Holy water is a purveyor of a mysterious force – an emissary for the power of the Creator. It is a symbol of cleansing and purity, and contains sacred life force energy. Holy water powerfully and instantly cleanses negative energy, and calls forth blessings and protection. Long recognized for its amazing powers of renewal and transformation in cultures around the world, holy water has been an integral part of Space Clearing ceremonies. Even in modern culture the spiritual cleansing properties of water are still acknowledged. For example, in some Catholic homes, a font near the front door is filled with holy water. Visitors dip their fingers into this and then flick the water into the room as a way of consecrating the energy there.

Holy water for Space Clearing

You can obtain holy water from a shrine or temple, or you can create your own. The potency of your holy water will vary with the source of the water, how it is made, and who makes it. The more sacred the stream or place from which it is obtained, the greater the water's strength. For example, water obtained from the Chalice Well in Glastonbury has wonderful and unique qualities. Additionally, the more powerful the intent, prayers, and mantras used when preparing the water, the more mystical it becomes. And, most important, the more spiritually attuned the person who blesses it, the greater the sanctity of the water.

You can make excellent holy water for your Space Clearing, if you prepare it carefully and with love. If possible, obtain your water from a natural source, such as a freshwater spring. This is one of the very best places to obtain water for Space Clearing as the water comes directly from the depths of Mother Earth. However, if you do not have easy access to a spring, you can use water which has been bottled at such a place. Any natural spring water that is "bottled at source" can be used, but it is better if the water you purchase comes in glass, not plastic, bottles. It is useful to note where the water came from, as it will retain energy imprints of this place. You can also use rainwater, but wait until it has been raining for a while as pollutants will be present in the first hour of the rain. Rainwater carries the lofty energy of the skies.

Once you have obtained your water, you need to "charge" it so that it is infused with robust energy for Space Clearing. Water gathered directly from a spring does not always need to be charged, because it still has the vibrant energy of the natural world in its essence. But bottled water does need to be renewed. You can do this in one of the following ways – the method you use depends on the project you have at hand. Bear in mind that water used for Space Clearing should be put in a glass or ceramic (not metal) bowl, as this can influence the energy of the water.

SOLAR-CHARGED WATER To capture the energy of the sun, place a bowl of water in the morning sunshine. Make sure the rays of light actually penetrate the surface of the water. Placing the bowl outdoors is preferable to a sunny window ledge, because the wind and essence of the outdoors will infuse it with extra vitality. It usually takes at least three hours for the water to become fully charged in this way. Solar water has a very *yang*, exuberant, sociable energy. It is wonderful to use when you want to add life and vigor to any environment.

LUNAR-CHARGED WATER Leave your bowl of water outdoors on a clear, moonlit night in order to infuse it with lunar essence. Lunar-charged water has a very gentle, healing nature which makes it particularly useful for Space Clearing after illness. It is also excellent for creating a restful energy in bedrooms and places of meditation. It is conducive to good dreams and incubating creative ideas.

STELLAR WATER Leaving water out to absorb energy from the stars on a clear night will give it a very special energy which is full of joy and magic. Star energy is at its most intense on nights with no or very little moon. The water that is instilled with star energy is wonderful for helping make dreams come true and bringing more rapture into life.

A FLOATING FLOWER
INFUSES SPRING WATER WITH
FRESHNESS AND VITALITY.

Flower essences to empower holy water

Another way to energize your water is by adding essences from nature, such as from flowers, gems, and shells. These essences imbue the spiritual properties of nature into the water. Research has shown that water has a "memory." This means that the essence of the spiritual properties of a flower, for example, can become imprinted into water. This is a type of vibrational alchemy.

Flower essences contain the pure spiritual essence of each individual flower. They are created by picking a flower at its peak in the early morning hours, and floating it in pure spring water while the sun shines on it. This is done in a meditative state to invite the energy of the flower into the water. Although you can create your own flower essences, usually the highest quality vibrational flower essences are those that have been created by people who have dedicated their life to this work. Bach Flower Essences, California Flower Essences, Australian Bush Essences, Perelandra Essences, and Alaskan Flower Essences are all companies of good reputation. I particularly like the Alaskan Flower and Environmental Essences because the Alaskan air is so clean and the land is so unpolluted.

When you add a few drops of flower essence to your holy water, it infuses it with the qualities of the flower. This kind of water can create a delicate web of energy which is very healing and conducive to inviting joy and love into a home. The flower essences you use will depend on the kind of energy you want to create. The following is a partial list of some essences and their qualities:

To bring calmness and peace into a home

CENTAURY   brings quietness, wisdom
CHAMOMILE   calming, soothing, good for a home that feels downtrodden
CHERRY PLUM   calming, quiet energy
LAVENDER   soothes tension and stress
MIMULUS   minimizes fear and dread
WATER VIOLET   gentleness, tranquillity, poise, and grace

To awaken mental clarity and focus in a home

BLACKBERRY   manifesting, directing action, decisiveness
CERATO   brings confidence and helps with decisions
CLEMATIS   dispels lethargy and ignites focus
PEPPERMINT   increases alertness
ROSEMARY   releases mental fog
SHASTA DAISY   focus and synthesis of ideas

To cleanse old patterns out of a home (e.g. after a divorce or trauma)

CAYENNE — breaking free of the old, catalyst for change
FIREWEED — the best essence for releasing old patterns and attracting new restorative energy
GORSE — positive faith in overcoming difficulties
RESCUE REMEDY — balances energy after trauma, argument, or illness
SAGEBRUSH — releases old habits that are no longer appropriate
STAR OF BETHLEHEM — clears residues of tension from past experience

To create a protective shield around a home

GARLIC — psychic protection for the home
PENNYROYAL — dispels negative influences
YARROW — strengthening, excellent for protection

To ignite energy and vitality

INDIAN PAINTBRUSH — stimulates creativity
PEPPERMINT — alert and vital
MORNING GLORY — reawakens vigor and new life
WILD ROSE — vitality, lively interest in all things

To summon spiritual awakening

ANGEL'S TRUMPET — deeply soothing and peaceful, spiritual initiation
ANGELICA — open to guidance from the divine realms
BLACK-EYED SUSAN — awakens consciousness
IRIS — spiritual integration
LOTUS — opens spiritual consciousness that has been restricted

SPIRALING WATER

Spiraling water strengthens its energy. Hold the water in your container and spiral it round and round. You can twirl the container, use a clean finger, or take a wooden spoon or stick to spiral it. This empowers the water. Water flowing in nature naturally moves in spiraling patterns. These spiral movements replenish the water's energy and increase its electromagnetic current. Still water or water flowing out of straight pipes does not have this vital essence, but you can restore it with a gentle swirling.

PRAYERS AND MANTRAS

The most important aspect of energizing holy water is through your prayers and reverence. Holding your right hand over the container of water, with your left hand held upwards, palm facing the heavens, imagine light entering into your left and pouring out of your right hand into the water. As you do this, add your prayers or mantras that the water be made sacred. This should be done in the early morning when the earth energy is freshest. Continue until you feel that the water has been saturated with Spirit. Know that every molecule of the water is now infused with the power of your prayers and your intention, and that whatever this water touches will be transformed.

Holy water needs to be treated and handled with respect. It must be kept in a clean container that has only been used for holy water. It is best to purchase a container for this purpose, although you can use any glass or ceramic container or bowl that has been thoroughly cleaned and dedicated for use with holy water. It should be stored in a place of honor such as on your home altar.

As you begin your Space Clearing, you may want to invoke the Spirit of Water to help you in your work. To do this, place a bowl of holy water on your Blessing Altar. Take a few moments to still your mind and fully connect with the Spirit of Water. Imagine a beautiful cascade of mountain water falling down steep stones to an alpine valley full of delicate wild flowers. This calls upon the Spirit of Water to bring the renewing energy of a cascading waterfall into your Space Clearing.

Below is an example of a prayer you could use to consecrate water:

May the Creator within all things fill this water with blessings and peace. May the water bring purification, healing, and love to this home and all who dwell here. So be it.

Casting Holy Water

One way to use holy water for Space Clearing is to dip a leaf, flower, or small branch in the water and then flick it into the space. In some ancient traditions, the shaman would carry a bowl of water in one hand. With his other hand, he carried a branch of herbs or a small sprig from an evergreen tree. This he would dip into the consecrated water and vigorously flick the end of the branch around the room, so that small drops of water were dispersed throughout the air.

To use this method, walk around the periphery of the room. Wherever you sense energy that is stagnant or negative, dip your small twig, flower, or stem into the water, and lightly but firmly cast the water into the area. If energy is really stuck then flick the branch seven times, wait a moment to sense if the energy has cleared, and if not, then flick seven times again. This method of flicking seven times is traditional in many cultures. Don't saturate an area – just a few drops is enough.

The plant or tree sprig you choose to use will subtly alter the effects of your clearing. Here is a partial list of some options you can try. You can also use your intuition to discover many others.

PINE BRANCH Excellent for clearing very heavy or negative energy. Extremely purifying and cleansing. Good for clearing after illness or depression, or when someone is feeling stuck in their life.

CEDAR BRANCH Shares most of the positive aspects of pine, but is somewhat softer in energy. Excellent for clearing spiritual energies.

LEMON VERBENA BRANCH Excellent for shifting the energy in a room quickly and for clearing negative energy following an argument. Increases mental clarity and perception. Leaves a vibrant, refreshing energy.

ROSEMARY Purifying and revitalizing, vibrant and emotionally warming, this is always a good choice.

ROSE FLOWER Good for working with very gentle energy, and for creating a delicate haven of love and affection.

DAISY FLOWER Especially good for clearing children's rooms and rooms devoted to sociability. A delicate tool best used to create environments filled with joy.

If you are clearing an area that has very delicate energy, such as a nursery for a newborn baby or very young child, you might want to use a flower for casting the water. In this case, you would use much gentler, softer movements of the wrist so as not to damage the flower or disturb the delicate protective web of energy you want to weave in this type of situation. Flowers are sometimes used to establish fresh new energy after a room has already been cleared with a stronger purifying tool, such as a pine twig.

It is also possible to clear a room using your fingers to flick water gently throughout the area. Doing this will feel very different from using a plant. You may receive energy vibrations as the water leaves your fingers that will help you to decide exactly which parts of the room you need to concentrate on.

MISTING A ROOM FOR PURIFICATION

Misting a room will instantly clear out stagnant emotional energies which have accumulated there. This is because negative emotions actually leave a kind of electrical charge hanging in the air which is rapidly cleared through the use of charged, essence-enriched water sprayed lightly throughout the room during a Space Clearing. An additional benefit of this method is that it leaves a healthy, negative-ion environment in the area when you are finished. (Negative ions increase mental alertness and uplift energy. They are naturally found next to waterfalls and in pine forests in nature, as well as at the shore. Misting is a way of re-creating these refreshing environments through Space Clearing.)

When choosing a water spritzer to use for misting, the finer the spray created, the better. There are many small beautiful bottles that can be obtained that work very well. The beauty of the mister is actually an important adjunct to its function, because it helps to consecrate the ritual. Select one which is comfortable to hold and has an easy-to-use spray mechanism.

The solution you use for misting in Space Clearing will be directly related to your intention. You will usually add a few drops of a flower essence or even essential oil to the charged water in your bottle. The ones you use will be a determining factor in the results you gain, so consider carefully. But don't feel overwhelmed. Your intuition is often more valuable than extensive knowledge. Just let go and trust that you will be drawn to exactly the best essences or essential oils for a particular clearing.

As with the flicking method, circle each room in a clockwise motion with your mister. Don't soak everything. Just send light puffs of mist into the air wherever you sense that the energy needs clearing. Misting is particularly useful for situations where negative emotions are at the heart of what is wrong with the energy. Doing this kind of Space Clearing produces immediate results. The room will feel lighter, fresher, clearer, and more positive.

BATHING FOLLOWING THE SPACE CLEARING

It is valuable to complete your Space Clearing by cleansing the auras of yourself and all the household inhabitants. Clearing a home without also re-setting the energy of the people who live there is like washing all your clothes but then forgetting to bathe your body! Using water for clearing the energy of the people who live in a space especially helps them to attune to the home's new energies.

After you have finished your clearing, ask the members of the household to take salt baths before they go to bed. (A few drops of rosemary essential oil or rosemary bath oil is an acceptable alternative.) Explain to them that as they bathe, they should visualize the new, fresh energy flowing through their homes. Tell them that they will emerge from their bath cleansed and revitalized and fully in tune with this new energy. If a bath is not available then briskly rubbing salt on the body while showering can produce the same effect. After the bath or shower, have a cold rinse.

CHAPTER SEVEN

Healing Earth

SALT AND RICE HAVE BEEN USED THROUGHOUT
HISTORY FOR SPACE CLEARING CEREMONIES.

Viewed from outer space, the Earth shines like a blue jewel set against a sea of jet black darkness. The swirling clouds of her delicate atmosphere drift in spirals of white, marking the orb like delicate veins on marble. The wonders of this planet were intuitively sensed by our ancestors, who worshipped her as the Mother Goddess, the foundation of life.

When you connect with the Spirit of the Earth in your Space Clearing, you are grounding your home to a primeval and powerful force for healing. The passage of the seasons, and the daily rhythms of our existence, are all lived in accordance with the cycles of the Earth. Her soil, her forests, her rocks and mountains, her plains and vegetation are the bounty that nourishes us body and soul.

Salt for Space Clearing

Salt is a gift from the Earth that has special significance for Space Clearing. Known throughout time for its remarkable purifying properties, salt in the ocean acts as an antiseptic to destroy bacteria. The ancient practice of tossing salt over the left shoulder to avert bad luck is based on the traditional use of salt to dispel negative energy. Because of its unique virtues, salt is one of the most essential elements in your repertoire of Space Clearing tools.

In performing purification for your own home, it is best to obtain natural salt, either sea salt or rock salt which has not been iodized. Which type of salt you choose will depend on your overall intention for the clearing. Sea salt will call forth the powers of the sea, which are especially conducive to cleansing and emotional healing. Rock salt on the other hand is associated with the powers of the Earth, and is very useful for achieving a sense of balance and grounding. These differences are very subtle, so use of either kind of salt will have a similar effect overall.

SALT PURIFICATION FOR YOUR HOME

There are several ways you can use salt in a Space Clearing ceremony. Placing a bowl of salt on your Blessing Altar while you are Space Clearing will help to ground and neutralize any negative energy you encounter as you work. You can also take a small bowl of salt and place it in the center of each room while you are clearing it. Or you can sprinkle salt throughout each room. Pay particular attention to the corners where stagnant energy tends to gather.

Salt sprinkled during a clearing should be left for 24 hours before it is swept up in order to allow enough time for it to absorb all of the negative energy. And salt used in Space Clearing should NEVER be eaten. It should be used only once and then rinsed down the sink followed by plenty of cold running water. Salt is used more than anything else in the world for Space Clearing. It is a universal purifier.

SALT, RICE, AND ASH

A traditional Eastern way to use salt for Space Clearing is to mix it with equal parts of rice to toss throughout a space. Additionally, in some traditions it has sacred ash mixed into it. Sacred ash consists of blessings which have been written (sometimes in special calligraphy) on paper and then ceremonially burned and added to the rice/salt mixture. The ash contains the essence of the prayers. You may want to write your own prayers and blessings on a piece of paper, burn it and mix the ashes with your rice and salt.

CRYSTALS FOR SPACE CLEARING

Clear quartz crystal, another gift from the Earth, is composed of silicon dioxide. Like salt, quartz is one of the Earth's most common and plentiful minerals. Used in Space Clearing, quartz crystals can act as generators of energy. Because crystals can be cata-

lysts for human consciousness, they possess the ability to distill, magnify and transmit your intention into a room. By placing a quartz crystal on your Blessing Altar, you will be able to deepen and radiate the energy field that you have created there. Natural faceted crystals can also be used as "wands" to implant sacred symbols into a room or to direct energy. To do this, hold an intention of a particular sacred symbol or ideal in your mind while directing the crystal in a particular place in a room (see "mystic symbols" on page 121). You can also simply outline the symbol in the air with the wand.

Cleansing your Space Clearing crystals

Regularly cleansing your clear quartz will keep it vitalized. This should be done after every clearing, or it will eventually lose its vibrancy. Here are several ways to cleanse your crystals.

SOLAR CLEANSING Place your crystal where the rays of the sun will directly fall on it. Leave it there for 3–4 hours. Then wrap it in black or dark purple silk to keep the energy intact.

SALT WATER CLEANSING Combine at least 1 cup of water with half a cup of salt. Embed your crystal in the salt before it begins to dissolve, and let it soak in the solution for at least 24 hours.

EUCALYPTUS OIL CLEANSING Holding your crystal in your hand, rub eucalyptus oil over its entire surface. As you apply the oil, begin at the base (this is the bottom or flat surface of the crystal) and work up to the top facet (the tip or apex of the crystal where all the sides come together).

Sacred dance for Space Clearing

Dance is an ancient way of celebrating our connection to the Earth. As the feet touch the ground, the body reaches for the heavens, thus establishing a sacred link between Mother Earth and Grandfather Sky. Your body can be one of the most exquisite and wondrous tools for Space Clearing. It can become your holy instrument to channel energy and light into a space. Tai chi or yoga classes can help you learn to use your body in a graceful way for channeling energy, but are not vital. Such classes can help you to get in touch with your physical form and understand how to sense and respond to energy with your body, but you can also simply use your intuition to find those poses and movements which are most expressive of Spirit for you.

To clear a space using your body, begin by standing at the entrance with your hands in a prayer position. Take a deep breath and exhale. Allow your awareness to expand so that you feel that you are filling every part of the room. Then step beyond your mind and all linear thought processes. Slowly allow your "body wisdom" to take over and begin to dance. Move, sway, flow. You might find your arms moving in a spontaneous spiraling movement in one area, and a soft pushing motion in another. Let your body become a sacred vessel for universal awareness to surge through the room. When you sense that the energy is balanced and complete, draw the sign of infinity in the air (a horizontal figure eight) to seal it in.

MUDRAS FOR SPACE CLEARING

When using your body as your Space Clearing tool you might consider the use of mudras (devotional hand gestures) to deepen the energy you are creating. The Sanskrit word "mudra" means "to seal." These graceful movements of the hands can be used to bless and seal the energy in a room.

Mudras have enjoyed a rich history since their emergence in Egypt. Following their early beginnings, the esoteric use of sacred hand gestures swept through the ancient world, and were used in Greece, Persia, India, China, and Japan. Particular hand gestures were used to actualize deep inner states. They allowed for an alignment of mind, body, and soul.

Today we can use mudras to implant and seal healing qualities into a living space. One simple mudra is performed by placing your hands in a prayer position in front of your heart chakra, the center of your chest. Imagine that heart energy is filling your hands and then allow them to move this loving energy into the room. Another mudra is performed by placing your left hand in your right palm with your thumbs touching. Cup them together in front of the center of your abdomen and imagine that you are filling your hands with light from this area of your body (which is called the tanden or hara). This creates very powerful grounding energy. Now lift your hands and send this energy into the room. Often when you are "dancing a room," you will form spontaneous mudras with your arms and hands. A deep wisdom is filling you at that time and each hand gesture is calling a needed energy into the room.

To deepen the effect of your mudras you may want to consider decorating your hands and feet with henna or felt markers. This time-honored practice is called mehndi, and the designs help to activate your energy. You can either obtain a mehndi kit, have yourself decorated professionally, or carefully create your own designs.

PENDULUMS AND DOWSING

The art of dowsing has been used for thousands of years to indicate energy fields. Prehistoric rock paintings in Algeria depict early dowsers, and

research has uncovered evidence suggesting that the ancient Chinese and Egyptians also used dowsing. The first written descriptions of dowsing appeared in the Middle Ages. Although there are many schools of thought regarding why dowsing is successful, practitioners of this ancient art all agree on one point: it works.

Many believe that dowsing works because dowsers subconsciously tune into the stream of wisdom available at the level of the collective unconscious of all people. The dowser receives information from this source, causing muscles to twitch, which in turn causes the pendulum to swing. In other words the body of the dowser becomes a receiving station to access the energy flows of the space around them. The dowsing tool acts as a focal point, or amplifier, for the information received.

You can use pendulums in your Space Clearing to detect energy fields as well as for clearing energy. Any weight attached to the end of a cord or chain can be used for pendulum dowsing. If you are purchasing a pendulum, find one that both looks and feels good to you. Before you begin to work with your pendulum, you will need to energize it. You can do this by holding your hands over it and imaging that light is radiating out of your hands into the pendulum. Energizing your pendulum usually improves the way it works for you.

To use your pendulum for Space Clearing, hold its cord or chain firmly between your thumb and index finger several inches from the pendulum – a comfortable range is usually between 3–12 inches (roughly 10–30 cm), so that it can swing freely and smoothly. Go through each room in your home, allowing the pendulum to swing in small circles. Anywhere that it begins to swing in wider circles can indicate the need for clearing. Allow the pendulum to spiral in that area until it begins to swing in small circles again. This indicates that the energy in that area has been cleared.

A SPIRAL OF STERLING SILVER FORMS A SAFE RECEPTACLE FOR A NATURAL CRYSTAL. ADD SOME CORD AND YOU HAVE AN INSTANT CRYSTAL PENDULUM.

MYSTIC SYMBOLS FOR SEALING ENERGY

Since the beginning of time, people have used symbols to express feelings of connection to Spirit, to the Earth, and to the multitude of life around us. You can implant the energy of a mystic symbol in a room, thus sealing the energy that you have created there. To do this, either outline the symbol in the air with your fingers or a wand, or else visualize it. When using your fingers, use your index finger and middle finger together. You can also draw the outlines of the symbol in the air using an elongated crystal or a wand. This will further imprint the energy of the symbol in the atmosphere of the environment.

Any symbol that has significance for you can be effectively used to seal the energy of a room. Use your intuition to discover which ones suit you best. You may find the following symbols useful:

TO EXPAND ENERGY IN A ROOM Make a spiral starting at the center and working outward.

TO PROTECT ENERGY IN A ROOM The five-pointed star (pentagram), the six-pointed star (the seal of Solomon), and the cross are all excellent to use.

CLOSING THE CIRCLE OF ENERGY Make a circle on each wall, and say, "The circle is now complete."

SEALING LOVE INTO A ROOM Visualize or draw in the air the shape of a heart. This is a contemporary symbol that is simple, but powerful.

GROUNDING AND REVITALIZING A HOME Draw a tree in the air, complete with roots and branches. By doing this you are planting the energy of the sacred Tree of Life in the home and this symbol will continue to ground and replenish the energy.

A Sacred Act

All life is energy. Physicists acknowledge that the atoms and molecules in all things are in constant motion. They declare what ancient mystics have always known – that beneath the surface of physical objects, energy swirls into form, dissolves, and coalesces once again. The world is in a constant dance of fluid patterns of ebbing and flowing energy. Underlying this motion is a cosmic order, an innate harmony in all life. However, as huge changes in technology have occurred, we have lost this fundamental balance in our lives.

The re-emergence of the ancient wisdom of Space Clearing is an organic and natural way to reclaim balance and harmony in our homes and in our lives. As you step into this sacred tradition you begin to experience that every object in your home affects your energy in a different way. The more you open up your heart and inner awareness to the realm of energy, the more you will hear the voice of everything in your surroundings. As you refine your ability to sense energy, you will notice when your home is out of balance, and you will intuitively know what is needed to restore harmony. This is an intuitive art, and like any art, the more you practice, the more refined your skills will become.

There is great power in small sacred acts. When you listen to your own inner wisdom, you will know what you need to do. When you Space Clear a home and call forth blessings for the people who live there, this is a sacred act. You are generating an energy field that will travel in ripples beyond the boundaries of the home into the universe around you, bringing a sense of grace, beauty, and love to all in ways that you may never be aware of.

When you clear and bless your home or business, this generates an extraordinary energy that radiates in all directions, positively influencing the surrounding area. Human beings are one small part of something grand and infinite, and even more wonderful than we can ever imagine. Though we are not often aware of it, when we open our hearts to the promptings of Spirit, this creates an energy that has an enormous impact on the universe around us. People you don't know and may never know will be influenced by what you do. Whenever you Space Clear you are making a difference in the world.

As you begin to understand the profound nature of Space Clearing, you will tap into an immense current of love, harmony, and profound power which assists us to be part of something much bigger than our individual identities. Space Clearing can help you connect with a divine force that can offer protection, purification, and blessings for your home, and ultimately for the world.

Space Clearing Resources

AUSTRALIA

NATIVE JOURNEYS
112 Auburn Road,
Hawthorne 3122, Victoria
tel: +61 (0)3 98 18 88 10
fax: +61 (0)3 98 18 88 09
http://www.nativejourneys.com
email: nativej@netspace.net.au
Handmade drums, rattles, sage, feathers, resins, charcoal, tingshaws, Tibetan bells, abalone shells, didgeridoos, Native American flutes, Space Clearing candles, click sticks, and essential oils. Call or write for catalog.

IN ESSENCE
3 Abbott Street,
Fairfield 3078, Victoria
tel: +61 (0)3 94 86 96 88
Excellent quality oils.

AUSTRALIAN BUSH FLOWER ESSENCES
Essential Energies,
54 Clifton Street,
Richmond 3121, Victoria
Flower essences.

UNITED KINGDOM

TISSERAND AROMATHERAPY PRODUCTS
Newtown Road, Hove,
Sussex BN3 ZRS
tel: +44 (0)1273 325666
fax: +44 (0)1273 208444
http://www.tisserand.co.uk
Essential oils. Available by mail order and from major health-food stores.

BACH FLOWER REMEDIES
Dr. Edward Bach Centre,
Mount Vernon, Sotwell,
Wallingford, Oxon
tel: +44 (0)1491 839489

WINDHORSE IMPORTS
PO Box 7, Hay-on-Wye,
Herefordshire HR3 5SF
tel: +44 (0)1497 821116
email: sales@windhorse.co.uk
Authentic and traditional tools, including drums, incense, offering bowls, prayer wheels, Tibetan bells, singing bowls, and tingshaws. Available by mail order.

ESOTERICA & THE FENG SHUI SHOP
5a Devonshire Road,
London W4 2EU
tel: +44 (0)20 8994 1414
fax: +44 (0)20 8994 0123
http://www.fengshuishop.com
email: info@fengshuishop.com
A selection of crystals, incense, and smudge sticks.

MYSTERIES
9-11 Monmouth Street,
London WC2H 9DA
tel: +44 (0)20 7240 3688
http://www.mysteries.co.uk
email: info@mysteries.co.uk
A selection of crystals, incense, smudge sticks, Tibetan bells, and Tibetan bowls.

RAYMAN
54 Chalk Farm Road,
London NW1 8AN
tel: +44 (0)20 7692 6261
fax: +44 (0)20 7692 5765
A selection of drums, rattles, and crystal shakers.

WILDE ONES
283 Kings Road,
London SW3 5EW
tel: +44 (0)20 7351 7851
fax: +44 (0)20 7352 3844
http://www.shop@wildeones.com
email: shop@wildeones.com
A selection of crystals, crystal singing bowls, drums, feather fans, incense, pendulums, rattles, Tibetan bells, Tibetan bowls, and tingshaws.

WORLD TREE MEND US
17 Station Parade, Kew,
Surrey TW9 3PE
tel: +44 (0)20 8332 0162
A selection of crystals, pendulums, and stones.

UNITED STATES

LIFETREE AROMATIX
3949 Longbridge Avenue,
Sherman Oaks, CA 91423
Superb quality oils specially formulated by John Steele. Information packet & order form can be obtained for $2.50.

ALASKA FLOWER ESSENCE PROJECT
PO Box 1369, Homer,
Alaska 99603-1369
tel (toll free in USA & Canada):
1-800-545-9309
tel (overseas):
1-907-235-2188
http://www.alaskaessences.com
email: info@alaskaessences.com
Outstanding Space Clearing combinations.

PERELANDRA FLOWER ESSENCES
P.O. Box 3603, Warrenon,
VA 20188
tel (toll free in USA & Canada):
1-800-960-8806
tel (overseas):
+1 (540) 937 2153
fax: +1 (540) 937 3360
http://perelandra-ltd.com
General supplies.

MYSTIC TRADER
1334 Pacific Avenue,
Forest Grove,
Oregon 97116
tel (toll free in USA & Cananda):
1 800-634-9057
tel (overseas):
+1 (503) 357 1566
fax: +1 (503) 357 1669
http://www.mystictrader.com
General supplies.

NUEVA LUZ
P.O. Box 31011, Santa Fe,
NM 87594
tel: +1 (505) 986 9163
fax: +1 (505) 455 1258
http://www.nuevaluz.com
email: nuevaluz@trail.com
Exquisite ceremonial smudging feather fans.

KAREN KINGSTON
http://www.spaceclearing.com
Balinese bells and other tools.

DAVID AND DENISE LINN
PO Box 75657, Seattle,
Washington 98125-0657
A selection of frame drums .

DENISE LINN
Courses and Training:
Denise conducts Space Clearing and Feng Shui training and professional certification courses in United States and occasionally overseas. For information write to:

Denise Linn Seminars
Interior Alignment
Professional Certification Course
P.O. Box 75657, Seattle,
Washington 98125-0657

Consultations:
Denise has personally trained professional Space Clearers who currently practice in 15 countries. For the name of a consultant in your area write to the above address.

Index

Acknowledgments

As always, I'm grateful to my husband David and daughter Meadow. These remarkable human beings continue to inspire and support me. Also thanks to Denise Bates, Claire Brown, Lisa Pendreigh, Nicky Thompson, Susannah de Amori, and Ruth Prentice for their wonderful editorial and design contributions.

All photographs in the book are by Sandra Lane except for pages 7, 37, 39, 41, 50-51, 56, 66 Shona Wood
page 11 Roderick Johnson/Link Picture Library
page 14 Pia Tryde
page 18 Michael Newton
page 55 Images Colour Library
page 97 The Photographers Library